ALL THE FULNESS OF GOD

THOMAS HOPKO

ALL
THE FULNESS
OF GOD

Essays on Orthodoxy, Ecumenism
and Modern Society

ST. VLADIMIR'S SEMINARY PRESS
CRESTWOOD, NEW YORK 10707
1982

Library of Congress Cataloging in Publication Data

Hopko, Thomas.
    All the fulness of God.

    Includes bibliographical references.
      1. Orthodox Eastern Church—Doctrinal and
controversial works—Addresses, essays,
lectures. I. Title.
BX320.2.H66   281.9   82-5454
ISBN 0-913836-96-6   AACR2

PRINTED IN THE UNITED STATES OF AMERICA

BY

ATHENS PRINTING COMPANY

New York, NY 10001

Table of Contents

All the Fulness of God

> *. . . that you may be filled with all the fulness of God.*
>
> — Eph. 3:19

The essays in this book all have the same theme. They witness to the conviction that human beings are made, together with everything that exists, to be filled with all the fulness of God. They claim that divine fulness dwells bodily in Jesus Christ, through whom God by His Spirit shares His life with the world. And they contend that fulness of life for creation—fulness of grace, truth, joy, love—is found by God's creatures in the Church of Christ "which is His body, the fulness of Him who fills all in all" (Eph. 1:23).

These essays in one way or another are about Christ and His Church. They are about what St. Augustine called "the whole Christ, head and body"—*totus Christus, caput et corpus.* They are about life in the Church, and the life of the Church, which is God's own life given in abundance in Christ and the Spirit as the life of the world.

The first article, "God and Man in the Orthodox Church," presents the theological vision. It is a revised version of a paper read at John Carroll University in Ohio as part of a summer program sponsored by The Walter and Mary Tuohy Chair of Interreligious Studies. It was published with the other papers of that year in a slim paperback entitled *God and Charity: Images of Eastern Orthodox Theology, Spiritual-*

ity and Practice (Brookline, Mass., Holy Cross Press, 1979). The essay insists that human life is fulfilled in knowing God, that such knowledge is genuinely possible, and that it is fully found in Christ and the Church. Already here the point is made that "the issue of the Church [understood as salvation and life] is the key Christian issue of our time . . . the most critical issue facing Christians today." Since God and the world come together in perfect communion in Christ and His body the Church, it follows, to affirm the ancient saying, "without the Church there is no salvation"—*extra ecclesiam nulla salus.* For without the Church there is no complete access to God in Christ and the Holy Spirit, no abundant fulness of life as it has been lavished upon the world by the tri-personal God.

The second essay, entitled "The Bible in the Orthodox Church," was originally written as part of a study project of the Orthodox Theological Society in America and published in *St. Vladimir's Theological Quarterly* 14.1-2 (1970). It is a "dogmatic" treatment of the Bible in Orthodox theology, *i.e.,* a statement of what the Orthodox Church, as Church, thinks and says about the Bible in her scriptures, liturgy, sacraments, councils and saints. The essay compares the theandric character of the Hebrew-Christian canonical scriptures with the theandric character of Christ and the Church, the point being that the truly *divine* can become truly *human* and in the process transfigure the human and render it genuinely and graciously divine. Thus God's Word can be incarnate in human words of various types and genres, just as the Word Himself can be incarnate in human form in His own person, becoming the real man Jesus Christ for the salvation of the world. Thus, once again, the human is "filled with all the fulness of God," becoming by grace what God Himself is by nature and thus becoming what it was originally created to be by its Master and Lord.

The third article is about the Church as such. It deals with the issue of "Catholicity and Ecumenism." It was read at the Second International Conference on Orthodox Theology and was published in *St. Vladimir's Theological Quarterly* 17.1-2 (1973) with other papers from the gathering. Here the theme

of Christ and the Church is specifically developed: God's
Son and Spirit have personally appeared on earth to bring
God's people and world into the fulness of divine being and
life in the unending Kingdom of God. The prologue of the
Gospel according to St. John, which is the gospel proclamation at the Church's eucharistic liturgy on Easter night, sums
up the message:

> And the Word became flesh and dwelt among us, full
> of grace and truth, and we beheld His glory, glory as
> of the only-begotten Son from the Father . . . and of
> His fulness have we all received, grace upon grace . . .
> (John 1:14-16).

The fulness of God in His Son and Spirit is in the Church
which is Christ's body and bride. Catholicity means fulness.
It is the quality of the Church which expresses her wholeness
and integrity. The Church is the mystical presence of the
Kingdom of God on earth. She is sacramentally constituted
within the space and time of this age in human structures and
forms, symbols and words, ceremonies and rites . . . all made
divine by God's action in His Son and Spirit. As such the
catholic Church is neither a denomination nor a sect. She is
rather the world itself, the whole of creation as fashioned,
redeemed, sanctified and restored by the power of God. The
"ecumenical" dimension of the Church's catholic character
and mission is understood in this light. It is the task of
rediscovering the Church's essential wholeness and integrity,
a task which first of all compels the Orthodox themselves to
judge their ecclesiastical structures, practices and policies as
they are historically conditioned and existentially actualized,
as well as to discern in others what is truly of God, and so
of the catholic fulness of the Church, and to affirm and rejoice
in it while at the same time revealing what is partial, defective,
merely human and plainly false wherever it is to be found.

The fourth article is entitled "Reflections on Eastern Rite
Catholicism." It is a revised version of an article published
some years ago in *Diakonia* 3.3 (1968). The essay presents
the author's convictions concerning the significance of Eastern

Rite Catholicism in relations between Rome and Orthodoxy and within the ecumenical movement generally. The essay argues that the real ecumenical issue among Christians is that of the unity of faith and life as expressed in proper theological definitions and terms, celebrated in proper liturgical and sacramental forms, and realized in proper behavior and action. Christian unity is not an issue of ecclesiatical authority as such. Still less is it a question of cultures, customs, rituals, mentalities, symbols or traditions in themselves. Once again the theme of all the essays presents itself. The essential question is raised: "What do you think of Christ? Whose Son is He? And everyone must answer, seeking the truth in terms of everything that one can know and appreciate regardless of its historical and cultural origin. . . . out of this will come the discovery of the unity of all people in God, in spirit and in truth."

In the spring of 1980 the author participated in a conference on *Eucharist With Children* sponsored by the Faith and Order Commission and the Office of Education of the World Council of Churches in cooperation with the Evangelical Academy of North Elbia, in Bad Segeberg, Germany. As a result he wrote two essays on the subject which in the present volume are combined into one called "Children and Holy Communion." The first part, published originally in *The Orthodox Church* newspaper (Sanatoga, Pottstown, Pa.) 16.11-12 (Nov.-Dec. 1980), consists in theoretical reflections on the subject. The second part, published here for the first time, presents practical considerations. The essay fits into the collection by defending the Orthodox conviction that "all the fulness of God" which embraces the whole creation in Christ and the Church can hardly exclude children so beloved of the Lord. From their very conception, and in a sense even before, God takes His children into His saving action and makes them full participants in the mystery of Christ and the Church, where they are received and consecrated at each stage of their growth "to mature personhood, to the measure of the stature of the fulness of Christ" (Eph. 4:13). The disorder in all the churches, including the Orthodox, about children and the sacraments—baptism, chrismation (confirmation), eucharist and confession—is a problem of major theological, spiritual, ecclesiastical and ecumenical importance. It is literally a life-and-death issue which must be confronted and resolved.

The sixth article in the book is about Orthodoxy and America and is entitled "Orthodox Christianity and the American Spirit." It was originally written for the bicentennial issue of *Spiritual Life* 22.1 (1976). The essay's purpose is to show how an Orthodox Christian vision of human being and life may be related to religious, spiritual and moral attitudes prevailing among modern Americans. A contrast is drawn between a way of life "filled with all the fulness of God" and ways of life determined by relativistic individualism on the one hand and sectarian collectivism on the other. The essay calls for a *method* of debate and competition between various ideologies and world-views in free societies which can overcome relativistic/sectarian "dead ends" in the pursuit of all that is true, honorable, just, pure, lovely, gracious, excellent and worthy of praise (see Philip. 4:8). It calls for "a Christian life in this new way which will be neither the peacefully coexisting conglomeration of relativistic individual and corporate opinions nor the crusading confrontations of self-righteous and closed-minded sectarians, but the free and gracious life of spiritual communion and conflict revealed to the world in Christ who offers the 'fulness of life' to those who receive Him in 'the church which is His body, the fulness of Him who fills all in all.' "

The final article in the collection is about "Witness and Service in Orthodox Christian Life." It was read at a conference on this subject sponsored by Syndesmos, an international fellowship of Orthodox youth organizations, in Montgeron, France, in 1979. The paper intends to show that the "insanity" which reigns among so many people today, especially Christians, can, once again, be overcome by the "sanity" of the "whole Christ, head and body," which is Jesus and His Church. The essay deals with the theological and spiritual malaise in contemporary Christendom and proposes an approach to its solution, using the specific issues of justice, freedom, identity and community to demonstrate an application of the Orthodox vision and experience to contemporary problems. The last essay concludes with the same point as the first: *The Church is the key.* She alone reveals the meaning of life because she is herself the "fulness of life" for those who have been blessed within her to be "filled with all the fulness of God."

The author is thankful to those who have permitted the reprinting of these essays and who have assisted in preparing them for publication in this present collection.

1

God and Man in the Orthodox Church

We have seen the true light.
We have received the heavenly Spirit.
We have found the true faith,
worshipping the undivided Trinity,
who has saved us.

—Liturgy of St. John Chrysostom

Many people come to the Orthodox Church expecting what Thomas Merton once called an "excitingly mystical excursion into the realm of a very 'mystical' and highly 'spiritual' religion, a gold-encrusted cult thick with the smoke of incense and populated with a legion of gleaming icons in the sacred gloom. . . ."[1] In the essay in which Fr. Merton wrote these words, he warned the reader that when he comes to see what Orthodoxy is really about, he may perhaps be highly "disturbed."[2] I would be quick to add that he may also be not a little disappointed.

It is my purpose in the pages which follow, if not to disturb, then certainly to disappoint those looking for any sort of "sacred gloom" in their interest in Orthodoxy. It is my task rather to present the fundamental vision of the Orthodox Church about God and man so that the reader might see

---

[1]Thomas Merton, "Orthodoxy and the World," *Monastic Studies* 4 (Advent 1966, Mount Saviour Monastery, Pine City, New York), p. 106.
[2]*Ibid.*

what lies behind the smoke and the gold and the gloom which fascinate so many and serve only to distract them from what Orthodox Christianity is really about.

The Knowledge of God

The fundamental affirmation of Orthodox Christianity is that God exists and that He can and must be known. Knowing God is, for the Orthodox, the only real purpose of life. Indeed, according to Orthodoxy, it is life itself. "And this is eternal life, that they may know Thee, the only true God, and Jesus Christ whom Thou hast sent" (John 17:3).

From her simplest parochial catechisms to the most sublime theology of her saints, and in all of her liturgical prayers and hymns, the Orthodox Church proclaims that God is not only to be believed in, worshipped, loved and served; He is also to be *known*. Centuries ago St. Athanasius, the great defender of Christian orthodoxy, put it this way:

> For what use is existence to the creature if he cannot know his Maker? How could men be reasonable beings if they had no knowledge of the Word and Reason of the Father through whom they had received their being? They would be no better than the beasts, had they no knowledge except of earthly things; and why should God have made them at all, if He had not intended them to know Him? But, in fact, the good God has given them a share in His own image, that is, in our Lord Jesus Christ, and has made even themselves after the same image and likeness. Why? Simply in order that through this gift of God-likeness in themselves they may be able to perceive the Absolute Image, that is the Word Himself, and through Him to apprehend the Father, which knowledge of their Maker is for men the only really happy and blessed life.[3]

[3]St. Athanasius, *On the Incarnation* (St. Vladimir's Seminary Press, Crestwood, N.Y., n.d.), p. 38.

It is characteristic of our time to deny that God can be known in any real sense of the term *knowledge*. Not only are there widespread and pervasive philosophical doctrines which claim that knowledge belongs only to "earthly things," to the world of the observable, the weighable and the measurable, and perhaps also to the realm of mathematical and logical forms; but there are also diverse sociological and even "political" and "psychological" positions which claim that any affirmation that God can be known necessarily opens the door to religious and ecclesiastical bigotry since it is tantamount to affirming that in moral, theological and spiritual matters some people are *right* and other people are *wrong*. There are even theologians today who insist that knowledge of God, strictly speaking, is impossible. They call for a plurality of "theologies" in which there is not only a variety of human expressions, concepts, symbols and words about God, but in which there is also a clear contradiction and opposition of meanings about who and what God is, and how He acts in and toward the world. This plurality of theologies, even of contradictory meaning, is defended on the basis of the absolute unknowability of God in his innermost being (the so-called *apophatic* character of God), as well as on the grounds that there are an infinite variety of expressions and manifestations of God in and toward His creatures, and an immense variety of situations and circumstances in which people make assertions about God's nature and activity through multiform categories of expression and explanation.

While affirming that God is indeed unknowable in His innermost being, and that there are indeed a multitude of manifestations of God and revelations in and toward His creatures, and that there are indeed an immense variety of forms and categories of expression and explanation proper to God in human thought and speech, the Orthodox tradition remains adamant in its insistence that not all of man's thoughts and words about God are "adequate to divinity" (to use a traditional expression), and that indeed most of man's ideas and words about God are plainly wrong, being, as they are, the inventions of the vain imagination of creaturely minds and not the fruit of a living experience of God in the actual reality of His self-disclosure.

It remains the position of the Orthodox Church, however it is judged and whatever are its consequences, that there is truth and falsehood in theological and spiritual matters, and that theology—certainly *Christian* theology—is not a matter of taste or opinion, speculation or erudition. Nor is it a matter of establishing the right philosophical premises and drawing the proper logical conclusions in the proper metaphysical categories. It is solely and exclusively a matter of giving proper definition to the mystery of God's being and action as God makes Himself known to His creatures, working salvation— as the psalm declares—"in the midst of the earth" (Ps. 74:12).

God can and must be known. This is the Orthodox testimony. God has revealed Himself to His creatures who are capable of knowing Him and who find their very lives in this knowledge. God has manifested Himself. He has not simply concocted some data about Himself which He has delivered, or some information which He has transmitted. He has made Himself known to those whom He has created in His own image and likeness for the express purpose of knowing Him, and all things in Him, and of delighting in this ever-increasing knowledge for all eternity.

The divine image and likeness in which human beings, male and female, are made, according to Orthodoxy, is God's own eternal and uncreated Image and Word, called in the scriptures His only-begotten *Son*. The divine Son exists with God in an exact identity of being, action and life, together with God's Holy Spirit. We have already met this affirmation in the words quoted above from St. Athanasius. The "Image of God" is a divine person. He is the Son and Word of the Father who exists with Him "from the beginning," the one in whom, through whom and for whom all things are made, the one in whom "all things hold together."[4] This is the Church's faith, affirmed in the scriptures and witnessed by the saints of the old and new covenants: "By the word of the Lord the heavens were made, and all their hosts by the spirit of His mouth" (Ps. 33:6).

[4] See John 1:1-3, Col. 1:16, Hebr. 1:2.

In the beginning was the Word, and the Word was
with God, and the Word was God. He was in the
beginning with God. All things were made by Him,
and without Him was not anything made that was
made. In Him was life, and the life was the light of
men (John 1:1-3).

. . . the Son, whom He appointed the heir of all things,
through whom also He created the world. He is the
reflection of the glory of God, the very image of His
person, upholding the universe by the word of His
power (Hebr. 1:2-3).

He is the image of the invisible God, the first-born of
all creation; for in Him all things were created, in
heaven and on earth, visible and invisible . . . all things
were created through Him and for Him. He is before
all things, and in Him all things hold together (Col.
1:15-17).

The way to the knowledge of God, according to the scriptures and the saints of the Church, is not by reasoning. God
cannot be reached by rational operations and logical deduc-
tions, though by such means people may be convinced that
there must be a God and that He ought to exist. God is
rather known by faith, by repentance, by purity of heart and
poverty of spirit, by love and by adoration. Which is to say
that God is known by those who are open to His self-manifestation and self-revelation, and who are prepared to yield an
existential acknowledgement of His power and action within
the world, which acknowledgement necessarily takes the form
of praise and thanksgiving (see Romans 1:18 ff). "He who
prays truly is a theologian," goes the often-quoted saying of
the ancient Christian tradition, "and a theologian is he who
truly prays."[5] In the words of St. John Climacus, "the climax

[5]The source of the saying is most likely Evagrius of Pontus. It is listed
in an English translation of the sayings from the Philokalia under the name
of St. Nilus of Sinai: Kadloubovsky and Palmer, *Early Fathers from the
Philokalia,* St. Nilus of Sinai, "153 Texts on Prayer," number 61 (Faber and
Faber Ltd., London, 1954), p. 134. At a congress of Orthodox Theological

of purity is the foundation of theology."[6]

> . . . the climax of purity is the foundation of theology.
> He who has perfectly united his feelings to God is
> mystically led by Him to an understanding of His
> words. But without this union it is difficult to speak
> about God. The engrafted Word perfects purity, and
> slays death by His presence; and after slaying death,
> the disciple of divine knowledge is enlightened.
> The Word of the Lord which is from God the Father is
> pure, and remains so eternally. But he who has not
> come to know God merely speculates. Purity makes
> its disciple a theologian, who of himself grasps the
> dogmas of the Trinity.[7]

Human persons know God when they preserve the original
purity of their nature as spiritual beings stamped by the uncreated Word and Image of the Father, being inspired by His
divine Spirit. Or rather, they know God when they uncover
and rediscover their original purity by God's gracious action
in and toward them through His divine Word and Spirit.
When persons live "according to nature" without corrupting
or perverting their being as the reflection of their Maker, the
knowledge of God is their most natural action and their most
normal possession. St. Gregory of Nyssa makes this point in
the following way:

> Now the divine nature, as it is in itself, according to
> its essence, transcends every act of comprehensive
> knowledge, and it cannot be approached or attained
> by our speculation. Man has never discovered a faculty
> to comprehend the incomprehensible; nor have we
> ever been able to devise an intellectual technique for

Schools held in Athens in August of 1976, no less than four of the speakers
quoted this text.

[6]See G. Florovsky, "The Ethos of the Orthodox Church," *Orthodoxy, A
Faith and Order Dialogue,* Faith and Order Paper No. 30 (WCC, Geneva,
1960), p. 41.

[7]St. John Climacus, *The Ladder of Divine Ascent,* translated by Lazarus
Moore (Faber and Faber Ltd., London, 1959), p. 264.

grasping the inconceivable. . . . (Yet) it is clear that the Lord does not deceive us when He promises that the pure of heart *shall see God.* (Matt. 5:8) . . . The Lord does not say that it is blessed to know something about God, but rather to possess God in oneself: *Blessed are the pure in heart, for they shall see God.* By this I do not think He means that the man who purifies the eye of his soul will enjoy an immediate vision of God . . . this teaches us that the man who purifies his heart of every creature and every passionate impulse will see the image of the divine nature in his own beauty. . . .

All of you mortals . . . do not despair at never being able to behold the degree of the knowledge of God which you can attain. For when God made you, He at once endowed your nature with this perfection. . . . You must then wash away, by a life of virtue, the dirt that came to cling to your heart like plaster, and then your divine beauty will once again shine forth. . . .

When your mind is untainted by any evil, free of passion, purified of all stain, then you will be *blessed* because your eye is clear. Then because you have been purified you will perceive things that are invisible to the unpurified . . . And what is this vision? It is purity, holiness, simplicity, and other such brilliant reflections of the nature of God; for it is in these that God is seen.[8]

What St. Gregory of Nyssa says here, which is a common teaching of the church fathers, is nothing other than what the apostle Paul has written in the opening lines of his letter to the Romans:

---

[8]St. Gregory of Nyssa, *On the Beatitudes,* homily 6, PG 44:1268B-1272C. See J. Daniélou and H. Musurillo, *From Glory to Glory: Texts from St. Gregory of Nyssa's Mystical Writings* (Charles Scribner's Sons, New York, 1961), pp. 98-102.

For the wrath of God is revealed from heaven against
all ungodliness and wickedness of men who by their
wickedness suppress the truth. For what can be known
of God is plain to them, because God has shown it
to them. Ever since the creation of the world His invisible nature, namely His eternal power and deity, has
been clearly perceived in the things that have been
made. So they are without excuse, for although they
knew God they did not honor Him as God or give
thanks to Him, but they became futile in their thinking
and their senseless minds were darkened. . . . And since
they did not see fit to acknowledge God, God gave
them up to a base mind and to improper conduct
(Rom. 1:18-21, 28).

The pure in heart see God everywhere—in themselves, in
others, in everyone and everything. They know that the
"heavens declare the glory of God and the earth shows forth
the work of His hands" (Ps. 19:1). They know that "heaven
and earth are filled with His glory" (Isaiah 6:3). They are
capable of seeing and believing, of believing and of coming
to *know* (see John 6:68-69). It is the fool who says in his
heart—exactly in his *heart*—that there is no God. And this
is because the fool is "corrupt, doing abominable iniquity."
He does "not seek after God." He is "fallen away." He does
not "call upon God." He has "no understanding" (Ps. 54:1-
4). The psalmist's description of the fool and the reason for
his folly have been summed up in the Church's patristic tradition in the conviction that the reason of every human ignorance is the willful rejection of God rooted in prideful self-
love.

According to St. Maximus the Confessor, the "original
sin" of human beings which infects us all, voluntarily and
involuntarily, is "love of self." Egocentricism enslaves its
possessor to the passions of mind and flesh and plunges him
into folly, darkness and death.[9] A person becomes blind be-

_____

[9]See Lars Thunberg, *Microcosm and Mediator: The Theological Anthropology of Maximus the Confessor* (C.W.K. Gleerup, Lund, 1965), pp. 164-
171, 327-342.

cause of his refusal to see, to affirm and to delight in what is presented to him, first of all the words and actions of God, and God Himself in His Word and Spirit in the world. This is Jesus' accusation, quoting Isaiah, when He says of the foolishly ignorant that they have eyes, but will not see; ears, but will not hear; and minds—but they refuse to understand.[10]

We must see this point clearly, and understand it well. The knowledge of God is given to those who want it, to those who seek it with their whole hearts, to those who desire it above all things and who crave nothing else (see Ps. 119). This is God's promise. Those who seek will find. There are numberless reasons why people refuse to seek and are unwilling to find, all of which, in one way or another, are rooted in prideful self-love, which can also be described as impurity of heart. The scriptural teaching, testified to by the saints, is that the impure in heart are blind because they prefer their own wisdom to the wisdom of God and their own ways to the commandments of God. Some of them, according to St. Paul, have a "zeal for God," but it remains unenlightened because they prefer their own righteousness to that which comes from God (Rom. 10:3). And these are they who victimize others through their propagation of folly which results in entire cultures and civilizations of corruption, confusion and chaos.

The reduction of the human being to something else, and something infinitely less, than a creature made in the image and likeness of God for wisdom and knowledge, and every divine virtue, is the greatest of tragedies.[11] The human person is made to be "God by grace." This is the Christian experience and witness. But the lust for self-satisfaction through self-affirmation in defiance of reality has resulted in the severance of human persons from the ground of their being which is God, and has thereby enslaved them hopelessly to the "elements of this age" whose very form is passing away.[12] There are any number of doctrines about human persons

[10]Isaiah 6:9-10; Matt. 13:14-17.
[11]See Vladimir Lossky, *The Mystical Theology of the Eastern Church*, (St. Vladimir's Seminary Press, Crestwood, N.Y., 1976), p. 124.
[12]Col. 2:8, 20; Gal. 4:3.

today which make them anything and everything but images of God; from the meaningless moments of some mythical historical-evolutionary process or material-economic dialectic, to the passive victims of biological, social, economic, psychological or sexual forces whose tyranny in comparison to the gods which they have allegedly destroyed is incomparably more ruthless and oppressive. And the fact that theologians, even Christian theologians, are there to provide their professional and professorial sanction to the enslaving power of self-contained and self-explained "nature" only adds further insult to this fatal injury.

But it need not be this way. And in fact it is not. Orthodox Christianity, or rather more accurately God and Christ Himself, are there to bear witness. The power for human persons to exercise the glorious liberty of being children of God is bestowed, preserved, guaranteed and cultivated by the living Lord who has made human beings to be, as St. Maximus has said, everything by grace that He Himself is by nature . . . if only they have eyes willing to see, ears willing to hear, and minds—and hearts—willing to understand.

The Knowledge of God in Christ and the Spirit

Whenever the true and living God is known and experienced, it is always by way of His Word and His Spirit. This is the teaching of the scriptures and the saints: ". . . no one has seen God at any time; the only-begotten Son who dwells in the Father's loins, He has made Him known" (John 1:18). "No one knows the Son except the Father, and no one knows the Father except the Son and any one to whom the Son chooses to reveal Him" (Matt. 11:27).

Whenever, wherever and however God is known, He is known by agency of His Son and His Spirit. Even the professed atheist, or the person who has never heard of the Father, Son or Spirit, who has the least inkling of something good, beautiful and true has in this sense—according to Orthodox tradition—known something of God; and that by means of His Son, who is His Word and Image, and His

Holy Spirit. Human nature is, by definition, the reflection of God. It is logical and spiritual; it participates in the divine Logos and Spirit. Every human being is imprinted by God's Image and inspired by God's Breath to manifest the divine in the creaturely form. Human persons can know and do good and create and govern because of their communion with their creator. Wherever and in whomever truth is to be found, God is there with His Word, who is the Truth, and His Spirit of Truth. Wherever and in whomever there is love or goodness of any kind, or beauty, or wisdom, or power, or peace . . . or any of the divine qualities and characteristics which belong perfectly to God, there God is Himself, once more by His Logos/Son and His divine Spirit.

Creation in its entirety, the heavens and the earth, the plants and the animals, everything that is, is made to be the created epiphany of the Uncreated Fulness, mirrors of the glorious splendor of God who has centered His creative activities and energies in human persons who are, by nature, "microcosms" embracing the fulness of creaturely possibilities, and "mediators" of all creaturely being and life before the throne of the Maker.[13] Once more we can hear Gregory of Nyssa on this point:

> For this is the safest way to protect the good things you enjoy: by realizing how much your Creator has honored you above all other creatures. He did not make the heavens in His image, nor the moon, nor the sun, nor the beauty of the stars, nor anything else which surpasses all understanding. You alone are a similitude of Eternal Beauty, and if you look at Him, you will become what He is, imitating Him who shines within you, whose glory is reflected in your purity. Nothing in all creation can equal your grandeur. All the heavens can fit in the palm of God's hand . . . and though He is so great . . . you can wholly embrace Him. He dwells within you. . . . He pervades your entire being. . . .[14]

[13]See Thunberg, op. cit.
[14]St. Gregory of Nyssa, On the Canticle of Canticles, PG 804A-808B. See Daniélou and Musurillo, op. cit., pp. 162-163.

When, because of sin in the perversion of his God-like
nature through prideful self-love, man plunges himself, his
children, his fellow-creatures and his world into ignorance,
folly and darkness, the Creator Himself acts to bring him
once again into communion with Himself. The Creator acts
as He always acts: by His Son and His Spirit, called by St.
Irenaeus the "two hands of God." He acts in His self-revelation in the law and prophets of Israel His chosen people. He
acts by His Word and His Spirit that they might know Him
and worship Him and find life in His name. And when
finally the human person appeared who was capable of fulfilling God's ultimate act of self-manifestation through her
total openness to the Lord, God's Son and Word was born of
her, the virgin mother Mary, and entered Himself into the
very substance of creaturely being and life in order to make
all things live by God's Spirit. This is how the Church proclaims it in her liturgical worship:

> For Thou, who art God inexpressible, existing un-
> created before the ages, and ineffable, didst descend
> upon earth, and didst take on the semblance of a ser-
> vant, and wast made in the likeness of man; for, because
> of the tender compassion of Thy mercy, O Master,
> Thou couldst not endure to behold mankind oppressed
> by the devil, but Thou didst come, and Thou didst
> save us. We confess Thy grace. We conceal not Thy
> gracious acts. We proclaim Thy mercy. Thou hast
> redeemed the generation of mortal nature. By Thy
> birth Thou didst sanctify the virgin's womb. All crea-
> tion magnifieth Thee, who hast manifested Thyself.
> For Thou hast revealed Thyself upon earth, and hast
> dwelt among men.[15]

This prayer, taken from the Orthodox liturgy of baptism
and read at the blessing of the waters, reveals the very essence
of the Christian faith: "And the Word became flesh and
dwelt among us, full of grace and truth . . ." (John 1:14).

[15]*Service Book of the Holy Orthodox-Catholic Apostolic Church,* I. Hap-
good, translator (Syrian Archdiocese, Brooklyn, N.Y. 1956), p. 278.

For what was God to do, says St. Athanasius, when He beheld man oppressed by the devil, if not to come and to save him?

> What was God to do in face of this dehumanizing of mankind, this universal hiding of the knowledge of Himself by the wiles of the evil spirit? Was He to keep silence before so great a wrong and let men go on being thus deceived and kept in ignorance of Himself? If so, what was the use of having made them in His own Image originally? . . . What then was God to do? What else could He possibly do, being God, but renew His Image in mankind, so that through it men might once more come to know Him? And how could this be done except by the coming of the very Image Himself, our Savior Jesus Christ? . . . The Word of God came in His own Person, because it was He alone, the Image of the Father, who could recreate man made after the Image.[16]

The Orthodox Church proclaims this, her essential faith, not only in the first great prayer of her baptismal liturgy, in and through which the human person is recreated, renewed and restored to his proper nature as made in the image of God; but she also places this affirmation at the center of her eucharistic thanksgiving in the divine liturgy called by the name of St. Basil the Great:

> For Thou didst not turn Thyself away forever from Thy creature, whom Thou hadst made, O Good One, nor didst Thou forget the work of Thy hands. Through the tender compassion of Thy mercy, Thou didst visit him in various ways. Thou didst send prophets. Thou didst perform mighty works by Thy saints who in every generation were well-pleasing to Thee. Thou didst speak to us by the mouth of Thy servants, the prophets, foretelling to us the salvation which was to come. Thou didst give us the law as a help. Thou didst appoint angels as guardians. And when the fulness of

---

[16]St. Athanasius, *op. cit.,* p. 41.

time had come, Thou didst speak to us through Thy
Son Himself, by whom Thou didst create the ages;
who, being the Radiance of Thy Glory and the Image
of Thy Person, upholding all things by the Word of
His power, thought it not robbery to be equal to Thee,
the God and Father. He was God before the ages, yet
He appeared on earth and lived among men, becoming
incarnate of the holy virgin . . . He emptied Himself,
taking the form of a servant, being likened to the
body of our lowliness that He might liken us to the
image of His Glory. . . .[17]

What the holy Church prays is what the scripture teaches.
Jesus Christ, the Logos incarnate, has come to deliver man
from demonic delusion and darkness, to liberate him from
his enslavement to the culture and tradition of sin, and to
transfer him once again into the kingdom of divine wisdom,
insight and light. The scriptures, especially the apostolic
writings, repeat this message again and again. The Wisdom
and Word of God has come to the world in human form,
in human flesh, and in Him dwells the "whole fulness of
deity bodily" so that in Him man might "put off the old
nature with its practices" and "put on the new nature which
is being renewed in knowledge after the image of the Creator"
(Col. 2:3-10, 3:9).

Jesus Christ renews human nature by sanctifying and
sealing it with the Spirit of God. It is by the Holy Spirit, the
Spirit of Truth who proceeds from the Father and is sent
into the world through the Son, that human beings come to
know God and to address Him with His eternally exalted
name of *Abba, Father.*[18] For the Holy Spirit takes what is
Christ's and declares it to men, bringing to remembrance all
that Jesus has said and done, and guiding His people into all
truth.[19] A modern Orthodox writer, the Elder Silouan (Sil-

[17]*The Divine Liturgy*, official translation of the Orthodox Church in America (second edition, St. Tikhon's Seminary Press, South Canaan, Pennsylvania
n.d.), p. 130-131.
[18]John 14:26, 15:26, 16:13; Rom. 8:15; Gal. 4:6.
[19]John 14:26, 16:12-15.

vanus) who died on Mount Athos in 1938, wrote this way
about the knowledge of God by the Holy Spirit:

> The Lord is made known in the Holy Spirit, and the
> Holy Spirit pervades the *entire* man: soul, mind and
> body. In this way God is known in heaven and on
> earth.
>
> If you would know the Lord's love for us, hate sin
> and wrong thought, and day and night pray fervently.
> The Lord will then give you His grace, and you will
> know Him through the Holy Spirit, and after death,
> when you enter into paradise, there too you will know
> Him through the Holy Spirit, as you knew Him on
> earth.
>
> We do not need riches or learning to know the Lord.
> We must simply be obedient and sober, have a humble
> spirit and love our fellow-men.
>
> We may study as much as we will, but we shall still
> not come to know the Lord unless we live according
> to His commandments, for the Lord is not made known
> through learning, but by the Holy Spirit. Many
> philosophers and scholars have arrived at a belief in
> the existence of God, but they have not come to know
> Him. To believe in God is one thing, to know God is
> another. Both in heaven and on earth the Lord is made
> known only by the Holy Spirit, and not through ordi-
> nary learning.
>
> Now the saints declare that they have seen God; yet
> there are people who say that God is not. No doubt
> they say this inasmuch as they have not known God,
> but it does not at all mean that He is not. The saints
> speak of that which they have actually seen, of that
> which they know. . . . Even the souls of the heathen
> sensed that God is, though they were ignorant how to
> worship the true God. But the Holy Spirit instructed

the prophets of old and after them the apostles and then our holy fathers and bishops, and in this way the true faith came down to us. And we knew the Lord by the Holy Spirit, and when we knew Him our souls were confirmed in Him.[20]

This doctrine of the peasant-monk of our day might appear as the anti-intellectual, anti-theological pietism of a man justifying his lack of education and learning and his separation from the worldly sciences by the mindless appeal to charismatic devotion and mystical illumination. But it is nothing other than the doctrine of St. Paul, the apostle to the gentiles, and St. John the Theologian, whom no one can accuse of lacking erudition. It is also the doctrine of the greatest theologians and intellectuals the Christian tradition, men and women schooled in philosophy, literature and all of the human and natural sciences of their day.[21]

The doctrine of Silouan may also be mistakenly taken as a radically individualistic teaching which can in no way be cast in objective terms. It may be considered as mere piety and prophecy, and not as theology, since it is considered to be devoid of scientific verification, lacking—as it is taken to be— in concrete historical, corporate, institutional and objectively-existing expressions and forms. The appreciation of Silouan's writings by the Orthodox, however, would be that he gives voice to a personal experience which is only possible if there

[20]Archimandrite Sofrony, *The Undistorted Image: Staretz Silouan, 1866-1938*, translated by Rosemary Edmonds (The Faith Press, London, 1958), pp. 115-118. This work, long out of print, was recently republished in two volumes by St. Vladimir's Seminary Press under the titles *The Monk of Mount Athos* and *Wisdom from Mount Athos* (Crestwood, N.Y., n.d.).

[21]The Cappadocian fathers, Basil and his brother Gregory of Nyssa and his friend Gregory of Nazianzus, the Theologian, as well as John Chrysostom, John of Damascus and Gregory Palamas were certainly educated in secular disciplines, yet their doctrine is that of the Elder Silouan. In our own time such men as Florovsky, Lossky, Bulgakov, Florensky, Verhovskoy, Schmemann and Meyendorff are all academically educated and not a few of them came to theology only after passing through philosophical, literary and scientific studies. Yet they too teach the doctrine of the peasant monk from Mount Athos. The well-known spiritual writer Archbishop Anthony Bloom, the Metropolitan of Sorouzh, living in London as the leader of the Russian Orthodox Church there, is still a practicing physician.

exists a corporate community within the time and space of this world which provides such an experience and gives it to all who enter into the reality of its life. For the Orthodox Christian this objectively-existing community exists. It is called the Church of Christ.

The Knowledge of God in the Church

The Christian Church, according to the Orthodox faith, is God's final and everlasting covenant of peace in the person of His Son Jesus Christ, the Messiah of Israel and the Savior of the world.

> Behold, the days are coming, says the Lord, when I will make a new covenant . . . not like the covenant which I made with their fathers . . . My covenant which they broke, though I was their husband, says the Lord. But this is the covenant which I will make with the house of Israel after those days, says the Lord. I will put My law within them and I will write it upon their hearts; and I will be their God, and they shall be My people. And no longer shall each man teach his neighbor and each his brother, saying, "Know the Lord," for they shall all know Me, from the least of them to the greatest, says the Lord. For I will forgive their iniquity and I will remember their sin no more (Jer. 31:31-34).

In the new covenant which God makes with His people in Christ, He Himself teaches them by putting a "new spirit" within them, which is His own Spirit, the Spirit of God.[22] In the Orthodox Tradition, the Church is defined as "life in the Holy Spirit" and the "Kingdom of God on earth" not in any purely "interior" and "mystical" way in the hidden life of the soul, but concretely and objectively in the sacramental and doctrinal life of the covenant community which is in-

[22]In addition to Jer. 31, see Ezek. 36:26-27; Ps. 51:10-12; Joel 2; Isaiah 42, *et al.*

carnate in space and time, locatable in human history, and living in this present age. The well-known Russian Orthodox emigré theologian, Fr. Sergius Bulgakov, put it this way in the opening words of his book *The Orthodox Church:*

> Orthodoxy is the Church of Christ on earth. The Church of Christ is not an institution; it is new life with Christ and in Christ, guided by the Holy Spirit. Christ, the Son of God, came to earth, was made man, uniting His divine life with that of humanity.
>
> The Church, in her quality of Body of Christ, which lives with the life of Christ, is by that fact the domain where the Holy Spirit lives and works. More: the Church is life by the Holy Spirit because it is the body of Christ. This is why the Church may be considered as a blessed life in the Holy Spirit, or the life of the Holy Spirit in humanity.[23]

This is also why St. Cyprian of Carthage could write centuries earlier that "he is not a Christian who is not in the Church of Christ," and "he cannot have God as Father who has not the Church as mother," and, most bluntly, "without the Church there is no salvation." For as Fr. Georges Florovsky has said, commenting on this text which he labelled a tautology, *"Salvation is the Church."*[24]

Salvation is the Church, and the Church is salvation, the gift of eternal life in the knowledge of God through communion with Him in His Son and His Spirit. This is the Orthodox faith. God Almighty acts in the world by His Word

---

[23]Sergius Bulgakov, *The Orthodox Church* (repr. Three Hierarchs Seminary Press, Maitland, Florida, n.d.—first published in 1935), pp. 9-10.

[24]St. Cyprian of Carthage, Letters 55 and 73, and *On the Unity of the Catholic Church*. Georges Florovsky, "Sobornost: The Catholicity of the Church," *The Church of God*, ed. Mascall (London, 1934), pp. 54-74. This article is also found in Florovsky, *Bible, Church, Tradition: An Eastern Orthodox View* (collected works of G. Florovsky, vol. 1, Nordland Publishing Company, Belmont, Mass., 1973). On this issue see also Vladimir Lossky, *In the Image and Likeness of God*, especially the chapter called "Tradition and Traditions" (St. Vladimir's Seminary Press, Crestwood, N.Y., 1974), and Thomas Hopko, *The Spirit of God* (Morehouse Barlow Co., Danbury, Conn., 1976).

and His Spirit, and He does so always through the community which He gathers. God always acts toward man as a whole. In the dispensation of salvation, which is the restoration of man's nature and the whole of creation begun in the Old Covenant and fulfilled in Christ's Church, God reveals Himself to a body of believers. He does not act toward isolated individuals. He does not reveal Himself to persons simply in the privacy of their souls. He deals with communities, His covenant communities, and the whole of mankind. If we ask the reason for this, the traditional Orthodox answer would be that God cannot act towards individuals in isolation because there is no such thing as an "isolated individual."

The "isolated individual" is the product of man's fallen imagination. It is a product of sin. It does not exist. It has no reality at all. What does exist are persons in community: people living together in the world in an identity of nature which cannot be broken except at the cost of man's perversion of reality and the destruction of his own humanity. What God has taught us in the manifestation of His Word is that we are of necessity "members one of another" (Eph. 4:25). It is interesting to note how even St. Anthony the Great, the father of monks and known for his seclusion in solitary confinement, has repeated this teaching in each of his letters:

> And He has gathered us out of all lands by the Word of His power, from one end of the earth to the other end of the world, and made resurrection of our minds (and our hearts), and remission of our sins, and taught us that we are members one of another.[25]

Man alone is not man. This is our teaching. Just as God alone is not God. The doctrine of the Holy Trinity at this point is of crucial significance. We have already indicated how, according to the scriptures and the saints, God would not be God if he were without His personal Son and Spirit, and how the witness of the Bible and the tradition of the

[25]*The Letters of St. Anthony the Great,* translated by Derwas Chitty (Fairacres Publication No. 50, SLG Press, Oxford, 1977), pp. 10, 15, 22, 25 and 27.

Church is consistent in its insistence that God Almighty has an only-begotten Son and a divine Holy Spirit in His very being as God. The eternal generation of the Son, Word and Image of God and the eternal procession of the Holy Spirit from the Father belong to God's being as God. If we seek a reason for this, the traditional response would be that the God who is Love could not possibly be God if He were alone in His divinity. He would not and could not be God if He were not an essentially self-communicating, self-sharing, self-manifesting being. A God without an eternally divine self-expression would just not be God and could not possibly be understood in any way as Goodness and Love. In more traditional words, a God without a personal divine Son and a personal Holy Spirit is not only not the God of the Bible known by the saints of the Old and New Testaments and glorified in the Church; he also would not be a God in any way logically and theologically comprehensible as living and acting in a manner which can be identified as good, generous, kind and loving. This means that multi-personality belongs to divine being and life as an absolute necessity. A uni-personal God, not to speak of an a-personal, supra-personal or impersonal God, is no God at all. He is the product, once again, of someone's fallen imagination: a creation of creatures. A God devoid of a personal Son, Word and Image and a personal divine Spirit would be the eternal prototype of self-containment, self-sufficiency, self-isolation and self-adoration. He would be the metaphysical archetype of the self-centered individual. He would not and could not be the perfect prototype of the self-sharing person who lives in communion with others in the union of love. As St. Gregory the Theologian put it when defending his "beloved Trinity" against the attacks of the philosophers with their allegedly perfect Absolute Monad: Our God is not simply *one,* but *communion.* And *communion* is far superior to mere *oneness* for it is perfect unity without the suppression of diversity and variety, and perfect multiplicity without the destruction of unity.[26]

[26]See V. Lossky, *The Mystical Theology of the Eastern Church,* pp. 46-64. *In the Image and Likeness of God,* pp. 13-139, *passim.*

God is not the supreme individual. He is rather the perfect person who lives in perfect inter-personal communion with other divine persons who are other than He, yet who are exactly what He is in the absolute unity of being, will, action and life. He is the Father, eternally and necessarily, the Source of divinity with His only-begotten Son who is also His Image and His Word, eternally born from His very essence in the "timeless generation," together with His "holy, good and life-creating Spirit" (to use another liturgical formula of the Orthodox Church), who eternally proceeds from the Father and shines forth from the Son, resting in Him as His very own Holy Spirit. The Church gives glory to the tri-personal Godhead in this way in the following hymn from the festival of Pentecost:

Come, let us worship the tri-personal Godhead,
the Son in the Father with the Holy Spirit.
The Father timelessly begets the co-reigning and co-
     eternal Son;
the Holy Spirit was in the Father, glorified equally
     together with the Son—
one power, one essence, one divinity.
In worshipping Him, let us say:
Holy God, who made all things through the Son,
     with the cooperation of the Holy Spirit!
Holy Mighty, through whom we know the Father and
     by whom the Holy Spirit came into the world!
Holy Immortal, the Comforting Spirit, proceeding
     from the Father and resting in the Son!
O Holy Trinity, glory to Thee![27]

Human being reflects the Holy Trinity. It is a plurality of human persons in the unity of one and the same identical human nature. And the Church is the restoration of human nature and the recreation of creation. This is the way that St. Gregory of Nyssa has said it:

[27]*The Vespers of Pentecost* (DRE, Orthodox Church in America, New York, 1974), p. 49.

The establishment of the Church is the recreation of
the world. In the Church there is a new heaven . . .
here too is a new firmament . . . a new earth is formed.
. . . Man is created once again, for by his rebirth from
on high he is renewed according to the image of his
Creator. . . . And there are many stars rising on the
firmament of faith. And there should be no wonder
that there are many stars numbered by God in this
world and called by name, for their names, says their
Creator, have been written in heaven. For it is in this
sense that I understood the Creator of the new universe
to say to His luminaries: *Your names are written in
heaven* (Luke 10:20). This is not the only striking
thing about the new creation . . . there are also a multitude of suns that light up the world with the rays of
good works. For thus does their Creator speak: *Let
your light shine before men* (Matt. 5:16) and again:
Then shall the just shine as the sun (Matt. 14:43). . . .
So too, anyone who looks upon the universe of this
new creation reflected in the Church can see in it Him
who is all in all, and . . . be led by our faith into an
awareness of the Transcendent. And so . . . [the soul]
shows how the whole Church is but the one body
of her Spouse (that is, Christ); and in her description
of His beauty she attributes a particular meaning to
each one of His members, but it is only by the union
of all of the particular members that the beauty of the
body is complete.[28]

The Church is the new creation. She is the union of many
persons, graced by God's Spirit, to be Christ's body and His
bride.[29] She is the experience, here and now in this age, in
time and in space, of the Kingdom of God not of this world,
the new heaven and the new earth of the new man in the
new Jerusalem foretold by the prophets, fulfilled in the
Messiah and His Spirit, and beheld in the mystic vision of the

[28]St. Gregory of Nyssa, *op. cit.,* 1049B-1052A. Daniélou and Musurillo,
op. cit., p. 273-274.
[29]Rom. 12:5; 1 Cor. 10:17, 12:12-27; Gal. 6:15.

Apocalypse as the very life of the world to come. And she is
not only total newness; she is total fulness as well: the participation in the humanity of Jesus, the incarnate Word, in
whom dwells the whole "fulness of deity bodily" and in
whom human beings come to the "fulness of life" (Col. 2:9).
For "of His fulness have we all received, grace upon grace"
(John 1:16). She is the Church which is Christ's body and
His bride, "the fulness of Him who fills all in all" (Eph.
1:23).

> He is the head of the body, the Church; He is the
> beginning, the first-born from the dead, that in every-
> thing He might be pre-eminent. For in Him all the
> fulness of God was pleased to dwell, and through
> Him to unite all things, whether on earth or in heaven
> . . . (Col. 1:18-20).

> For He has made known to us in all wisdom and in-
> sight the mystery of His will, according to His pur-
> pose which He set forth in Christ as a plan for the
> fulness of time, to unite all things in Him, things in
> heaven and things on earth . . . and He has put all
> things under His feet and has made Him the head
> over all things for the Church, which is His body, the
> fulness of Him who fills all in all (Eph. 1:9-10,
> 22-23).

There is an urgent need today for Christians to rediscover
the Church. There is a critical need to go beyond all the
rhetoric about theologies and traditions, beyond all claims
about the contributions and enrichments of the many sects
and denominations, and to discover again the reality of the
"household of God, which is the Church of the living God,
the pillar and bulwark of the truth" (1 Tim. 3:15).

God has established His final and everlasting covenant
with human beings in His Son, the Messiah. What the
prophets have predicted has come to pass. The covenant in
the blood of the Son of God, the living temple animated by
the Spirit of God, is with us. God is with us. The virgin has

conceived and borne a child. Jesus Christ has come and established His Church and "the gates of hell shall not prevail
against it" (Matt. 16:18).

The Church of the living God exists on earth. It is not
some invisible ideal far off in the heavens. Neither is it a
conglomeration of competing and contradicting denominations and sects. Nor is it a charismatic fellowship of believers
singing of their unity in the Spirit, despite all evidence to
the contrary. Nor is it a company of confessional families,
each one confessing in its own peculiar way. Nor is it some
sort of divinely established organization ruled on earth by
sacerdotal potentates serving up infallible decrees and moral
pronouncements for the spiritual benefit of their subjects. It
is the Church of the living God; the Bridegroom with His
bride; the Head with His body; the True Vine with His
branches; the Chief Cornerstone with His living stones built
into an animated temple in the sovereign freedom of the
Spirit of God; the Great High Priest offering Himself and
those with Him as the perfect sacrifice to the Father; the
King of God's Kingdom together with all those who reign
in and with Him; the Good Pastor with His reasonable flock;
the Master with His disciples; God with man and man with
God in the perfect communion of truth and love, in the perfect unity of being and life, in the perfect liberty of the life-
creating Trinity.

The Church of the living God is a sacramental community.
It exists as an objective, historical reality in the midst of the
earth. It is one with the unity of God. It is holy with His
holiness. It is catholic with the boundless fulness of His
divine being and life. It is apostolic with His own divine
mission. It is eternal life, God's Kingdom on earth, salvation
itself.

There is a gracious humanity to the Church. It could
hardly be otherwise, for it is humans who are being saved.
But the humanity of the Church, like the humanity of Jesus,
is not a "mere humanity." It is certainly not a sinful humanity. It is the divine humanity of the Godman Christ communicated by the grace of God's Spirit. It is man's original
humanity made perfect by God. It is the only humanity that

we know, the only one which exists: restored, resurrected, renewed, recreated. It is the humanity of Christ into which people are born on the day of their baptism, chrismation and first participation in the holy eucharist.

A person enters the Church by dying and rising with Christ in the baptismal mystery which, in the Orthodox tradition, is called "holy illumination." The baptismal fount, St. Cyril of Jerusalem has said, is the tomb and the womb, the grave and the mother.[30] Persons die in the baptismal waters with Jesus in order to be born into the new humanity of the Kingdom of God. They die with Him in the fount to the demon-riddled and deathbound life of this age in order to live with Him already *now* in the eternal life of the age to come. Immediately following baptism, accomplished by threefold immersion in the name of the Trinity, the "newly-enlightened" is clothed with the white robe of salvation and receives, through the anointing with sacred chrism, the "seal of the gift of the Holy Spirit."[31] This is the person's personal pentecost, as baptism is his personal pascha. The person receives God's Spirit in order to be capable of living the life of God into which he is born in baptism. And immediately following the sacrament of chrismation (understood quite differently from the *confirmation* of most Western Christians), the neophyte, even when an infant, is led immediately to the eucharistic table to partake of the Bread of Life, the body and blood of Christ, in the marriage supper of the Lamb of God in the Kingdom of heaven.

In the Orthodox tradition, the Church, as we have seen, is called the "Kingdom of God on earth." She is the Kingdom of the Father because she is the bride of the Son whose life consists in communion with the divine nature which is experi-

---

[30]St. Cyril of Jerusalem, *Lectures on the Christian Sacraments* (St. Vladimir's Seminary Press, Crestwood, N.Y., 1977), p. 61.

[31]*Service Book, ed. cit.,* p. 281. See 2 Cor. 1:22; Eph. 1:13, 4:30. For a summary of patristic interpretations of the sacramental mysteries of the Church see J. Daniélou, *The Bible and the Liturgy* (Notre Dame, Indiana, 1956). For a contemporary Orthodox interpretation see Alexander Schmemann, *For the Life of the World* (St. Vladimir's Seminary Press, Crestwood, N.Y., 1963) and *Of Water and the Spirit* (St. Vladimir's Seminary Press, Crestwood, N.Y., 1974).

enced by creatures as "righteousness and peace and joy in the Holy Spirit" (Rom. 14:17).

> His divine power has granted us all things that pertain to life and godliness, through the knowledge of Him who called us to His own glory and excellence, by which He has granted to us His precious and very great promises, that through these you may escape from the corruption that is in the world because of passion, and become partakers of the divine nature (2 Pet. 1:3-4).

In the Church of Christ human persons enter paradise and become partakers of the nature of the Holy Trinity. The Church's eucharistic sacrifice is the all-embracing act of her self-realization as a sacramental community. As such, the eucharist is the expression of the very substance of the Church as salvation itself. The Church is salvation because her very being is communion with God, and with all things in Him, "things in heaven and things on earth."[32] In the Church human beings participate in the divine liturgy of the Trinity, the "common action" of the three divine persons: Father, Son and Holy Spirit. (The word *liturgy* means *common action*.) They join the celestial liturgy of the angels, entering into the ceaseless singing of the thrice-holy hymn to the Creator. They join in the cosmic liturgy, participating with the heavens and the earth and all of the creatures in "blessing the Lord" and "proclaiming the glory of God."[33] They enter a reality incomparably more fearful and glorious than even that "terrifying sight" upon the mountaintop which caused the ancient Moses to "tremble with fear."

> But you have come to Mount Zion and to the city of the living God, the heavenly Jerusalem, and to innumerable angels in festal gathering, and to the assembly [literally: *church*] of the first-born who are enrolled

[32]Eph. 1:10; Col. 1:20. See also Nicholas Cabasilas (1322-1387), *The Life in Christ* and *A Commentary on the Divine Liturgy* (St. Vladimir's Seminary Press, (Crestwood, N.Y., 1974 and 1977).

[33]Ps. 19:1, 50:6, 69:34, *et al.* Also the Song of the Three Youths.

in heaven, and to a judge who is God of all, and to
the spirits of just men made perfect, and to Jesus, the
mediator of a new covenant, and to the sprinkled blood
that speaks more graciously than the blood of Abel.
. . . Therefore let us be grateful for receiving a kingdom which cannot be shaken, and thus let us offer to
God acceptable worship, with reverence and awe, for
our God is a consuming fire (Hebr. 12:22-28).

This, after all, is what Thomas Merton's "gold-encrusted
cult thick with the smoke of incense and populated with a
legion of gleaming icons" is all about. It manifests the fact
that God is with us and we are with Him, with all of the
angels and saints and the whole of creation, in a "kingdom
which cannot be shaken." Everything in the Church—not only
the icons and the incense, but also the songs and the hymns,
the dogmas and the prayers, the vestments and the candles,
the processions and the prostrations—bears witness to the fact
that the Church is *salvation*: communion with God in His
redeemed, resurrected, transfigured and glorified creation.
Everything proclaims the fact that the Messiah has come,
that God is with us, and that all things have been made new.
Everything cries out with the fact that "through Him we
have access in one Spirit to the Father" and are "no longer
strangers and sojourners, but . . . fellow citizens with the
saints and members of the household of God . . . Christ
Jesus Himself being the cornerstone, in whom the whole
structure is joined together, and grows into a holy temple in
the Lord . . . a dwelling place of God in the Spirit" (Eph.
2:18-22).

In the Church's divine liturgy we see why the world was
made. We see God and man as they are meant to be seen.
We have the vision granted to St. John in the Apocalypse.
And more than the vision. We have the reality. We have
salvation.

There are many theories about salvation today. Some are
cast in individualistic terms and have to do with people's
"souls." Others are collectivistic in nature, and have to do
with "history" or "society" or the "cosmos" or the "process."

Virtually all of them posit a radical dichotomy between this world and the age to come. And virtually none of them see the Church as the sacramental experience of God's good world made good again in Christ and the Spirit as the Kingdom of God. The world is all too often defined today even by theologians as an end in itself: a "dead end" to be rejected and scorned, or a glorious end to be affirmed in itself as all that we have. And the age to come is all too often thought of as a reality totally alien to the life of this world, a reality scorned and rejected by some as intolerable "pie in the sky," while being adored by others as the radical, antithetical answer to this "vale of tears." For the true Church of Christ, however, such dichotomies are impossible. And in the Church of Christ they are, happily, most gloriously overcome.

God made the world and He called it "very good." God loves the world which He made, and He does everything He can to save it by sending His only-begotten Son to be its life when it has become perverted, corrupted and dead. The Church not only proclaims this gospel; she also "prays" it in her liturgies and sacramental mysteries. (We have seen this already in our citation of the baptismal and eucharistic texts.) God saves the world which He loves as the body and bride of His Son who empties Himself for His beloved in order to become all that she is: creaturely, cursed, sinful and dead, in order to make her to be all that He is: divine, holy, righteous and everlastingly alive.

God does not bless and affirm the world in its rebellion and corruption. Nor does He scorn and reject it in its wickedness and sin. He simply loves it and saves it. And, once more, the Church is this salvation. It is the world redeemed by its divine Lover and Lord. It is the world experienced as God's Kingdom for those who have eyes to see, ears to hear and minds willing to understand. It is the Kingdom revealed here and now by the presence of Christ in the Spirit.

> What no eye has seen, nor ear heard, nor the heart of man conceived, what God has prepared for those who love Him, God has revealed to us through the Spirit (1 Cor. 2:9-10).

The issue of the Church is the key issue of our time. It is the most critical issue facing Christians today. It is the issue the resolution of which will decide the fate not only of Christians and Christianity, but of creation itself. The choice before us today is between a Christianity of substance and power, a Christianity of objective truth and universal significance, or a Christianity of taste and opinion, of subjective assertion and scholarly disputation. The choice is between a Christianity of Christ and the Church and the Kingdom of God, or a Christianity construed as but one of the many "religions" of the fallen world, and even that in a variety of contradictory versions and forms.

A modern author (I believe it was Chesterton) has written that when a person ceases to believe in the true God, and so in His Church, he believes not in *nothing;* he believes rather in *anything.* How many "anythings" there are today, not a few of which bear the name of Christian, even Orthodox Christian. The mutation of Christianity from the objective reality of the Church as God's Kingdom in the world into the great variety of "anythings" which now abound is the greatest of tragedies. It began with the distortions produced by theologies born not out of the living experience of God in the Church, but from the imagination of men's minds. These theologies in turn produced distortions in the sacramental and spiritual life of the community which have brought us to the present darkness and chaos in which we find ourselves wandering.

Distorted visions of God produce distorted experiences in the Church, and distorted Church experiences reproduce distorted visions. And the circle progresses in the endless production of distorted visions and experiences of human being and life. We live with them today. They are rooted in Christian soil, but now they violently oppose their own foundations. They are, as has been said, Christianity gone mad! And there are those who would consecrate the madness with references to richness, variety, diversity, catholicity . . . and even Pentecost! But the more pertinent reference is rather to Babel, as the liturgical hymn of the festival itself declares:

When the Most High came down and confused the
    tongues
He divided the nations.
But when He distributed tongues of fire,
He called all people to unity.
Therefore with one voice we glorify the All-Holy
    Spirit.[34]

Life in the Spirit

Our time is one in which many people are interested in
the spiritual life. Spirituality is *in.* If we knew history better,
we might have predicted it. There seems to be a pattern.
After a period of rampant secularism, a season of civil strife,
a time of exhausting the senses in search of satisfaction, there
inevitably follows a time of religious revivalism and a season
of interest in things "spiritual." One wonders which of the
two is more welcome: secularism or spiritualism? Especially
in a culture where Christ and the Spirit are separated from
the Church experienced as a liturgical, sacramental community
with its scriptures, dogmas, canons and saints. Christian
spiritual life without the objective reality of the Church in
which this life is lived—the Church which *is* life—is condemned in advance to frustration and failure. It cannot help
but be a fragmented and distorted experience of life, a mixture of many things, some of darkness and some of light,
unable ultimately to handle and to satisfy the whole of
human experience. Spiritual life without the Church, even
when people take the Bible for their guide, cannot but be an
unwholesome affair. It can hardly fail to be an experience of
being "tossed to and fro, and carried about by every wind of
doctrine, by the cunning of men, by their craftiness in deceit-
ful wiles" (Eph. 4:14).
    To make such a claim is not at all to say that the millions
of human beings outside the communion of the Orthodox
Church are devoid of God's grace and are automatically shut
out of the Kingdom of heaven. God's grace surely extends

[34]Kontakion of Pentecost.

beyond the earthly boundaries of the Church taken as a canonical organization. This is an Orthodox dogma. The Spirit of God "blows where He wills." Christ is not a prisoner of His own Church. He is the Lord of the entire universe. He is the Master of all. He enlightens every person who comes into the world. He desires all people to be saved and to come to the knowledge of the truth. He works to that end with all of His divine power and love.

It is also a dogma of the Orthodox that mere membership in the Church is no guarantee of salvation. The Church is salvation, but a person may partake of her saving life unto condemnation and judgment. This happens when a person participates in the sacramental life of the community without actually struggling to live that life in its fulness at every moment of his existence.[35] It is even the case that persons who persist in going through the motions of churchly life while resisting God's grace in actuality will inevitably become worse instead of better, darker instead of lighter, "more dead" instead of more filled with life. They will become angry, bitter, suspicious, resentful, jealous, judgmental and spiritually destroyed. "It is a fearful thing to fall into the hands of the living God," for our God is indeed "a consuming fire" (Hebr. 10:31, 12:29).

The spiritual life, according to Christian Orthodoxy, is the personal acquisition and application of that which is sacramentally given in the gracious life of the Church. It is the personal doing of that which is done by the Church in her mystical life and activity. It is the realization of the Church's liturgy in daily life. It is the transfiguration of the routine drudgery of the "every day" into the abiding paradise of the Day of the Lord. It is the continuous effort to apply what is prayed and proclaimed. It is, in a word, an ascetic effort made possible by faith and by grace, a perpetual dying and rising with Jesus, a continual reception of the Holy Spirit, a ceaseless spiritual communion in the marriage supper of the

[35]The prayer at the Orthodox Divine Liturgy before the reception of Holy Communion says: "Not unto judgment, nor unto condemnation be my participation in Thy Holy Mysteries, O Lord, but for the healing of soul and body."

Lamb. And, as such, it is the crucifixion of the flesh with its passions and desires. It is the taking up and bearing of the Cross, without which one is neither Christian nor human, and certainly not *divine*.

No one in the Orthodox calendar of saints is more "charismatic" and "mystical" than St. Simeon the New Theologian. The following passage from his spiritual teachings is characteristic of Orthodoxy (to refer once again to Thomas Merton) as a "very 'mystical' and highly 'spiritual' religion":

> The only thing that God demands of us mortals is that we do not sin . . . this is merely keeping inviolate the image and high rank we possess by nature. Clothed thus in the radiant garments of the Spirit, we abide in God and He in us. Through grace we become gods and sons of God and are illumined by the light of His knowledge. . . .

> It is right that we should first of all bend our necks to the yoke of Christ's commandments . . . walking in them and zealously even unto death renewing ourselves forever and making of ourselves a fresh paradise of God until, through the Holy Spirit, the Son and the Father enter into us and dwell in us.

> Let us look then how to glorify God. The only way we can glorify Him is as the Son has glorified Him. . . . But by that, by which the Son has glorified His Father, was the Son Himself glorified by the Father. Let us then strive to do what the Son has done. . . .

> This is the Cross—to become dead to the whole world; to suffer sorrows, temptations, and other passions of Christ. In bearing this cross with complete patience, we imitate Christ's passion and thus glorify our God the Father as His sons in grace, co-heirs of Christ.[36]

[36]St. Simeon the New Theologian, *Practical and Theological Precepts* 48, 107 and 114, quoted from *Writings from the Philokalia on Prayer of the*

This is the traditional "spirituality" of the Orthodox Church. This is the way through which God is known and glorified, the way through which the human person finds and fulfills himself as God's creature. It is the way of self-emptying love. It is the way ultimately of *suffering.*

Orthodox spirituality is the spirituality of suffering, or rather, more accurately, of co-suffering love. It is the way in which a person is made perfect, for it is the way in which Christ Himself was perfected in His humanity.

> But we see Jesus . . . crowned with glory and honor because of the suffering of death, so that by the grace of God He might taste death for every one. For it was fitting that He . . . should make the pioneer of their salvation perfect through suffering. . . . Although He was a Son, He learned obedience through what He suffered; and being made perfect He became the source of eternal salvation to all who obey Him (Hebr. 2:10, 5:7).

Why is it that the Messiah, God's incarnate Son, is Himself made perfect through suffering? The answer can only be, as Jesus Himself taught, that perfection is love; and love in the fallen world is inevitably suffering. It cannot be otherwise. Love is also the reason why persons can find themselves only by losing themselves for others; fulfill themselves by emptying themselves for others; discover themselves by forgetting themselves for others. This too is why the only truly free people are those who serve others; the only rich are those who have made themselves poor; the only powerful, those who are meek in overcoming evil solely by good. This is why, finally, a human being only really lives when he is willing and able to die to himself in every way, for death in "this world" is the perfection of giving, and giving is God's very nature and life as Love.

We already reflected on the fact that God Almighty is an essentially self-sharing being. We saw how, according to

Heart, translated by Kadloubovsky and Palmer (Faber and Faber Ltd., London, 1951), pp. 48, 122-124.

Orthodox experience and understanding, a God who would be enclosed in His own individual existence could not be the God who is Love. It is this essential self-sharing of God that is manifested in all its majesty and glory in Christ on the Cross. And it is the total self-sharing of Jesus in the humanity which God's Son has assumed "for us men and our salvation," that makes His humanity perfect and the source of perfection for all.

There is no "tragedy" in the eternal self-sharing of God in the inner trinitarian being and life. And there will be no "tragedy" in the self-sharing love which constitutes the very life of the Kingdom of God to come. But in "this world" which is fallen, whose prince is the devil and whose form is passing away, the perfection of love is always a cross, a terrible tragedy, but one that is transformed into victory and glory in the person of Christ.

The content of eternal life and perfection—and so the content of Orthodox spirituality—is co-crucifixion with Christ in co-suffering love for the sake of truth. This is the meaning of Jesus' "new commandment" that we should love one another as He has loved us. It is not simply one more commandment to love. Love is an "old commandment," one that we have from God "from the beginning" (see 1 John 1:7, 3:11). The new commandment given to the new creation is to love with God's own love, which is the love which the Father has poured into our hearts by His own Holy Spirit.

> . . . and we rejoice in our hope of sharing the glory of God. More than that, we rejoice in our sufferings, knowing that suffering produces endurance, and endurance produces character, and character produces hope, and hope does not disappoint us, because God's love has been poured into our hearts through the Holy Spirit who has been given to us (Rom. 5:2-5).

The one true and living God is the God who is Love, and being Love He suffers in us, with us and for us in His Son by His Spirit. Every human being is made in the image and according to the likeness of this God who is Love, whose own uncreated, divine image is His only-begotten Son sent into the world as Jesus Christ, the "son of His love" to be crucified (Col. 1:13). The perfection of the human person and the very substance of human spiritual life is to partake of God's nature and to share in His life. And in this world this means always and of necessity to share in His sufferings, joyfully and gladly.

This is the essential vision of God and man in the Orthodox Church. It is the vision of God crucified in the flesh in love for the world so that His creatures, by their own co-suffering love in and with Him, might themselves become all that He is. This vision is fulfilled and perfected on the Cross. It is revealed in the lives of God's saints.

Therefore since we are surrounded by so great a cloud of witnesses, let us also lay aside every weight and sin which clings so closely, and let us run with perseverance the race that is set before us, looking to Jesus the author and perfecter of our faith, who for the joy set before Him endured the Cross, despising the shame, and is seated at the right hand of the throne of God. Consider Him who endured from sinners such hostility against Himself, so that you may not grow weary or fainthearted. In your struggle against sin you have not yet resisted to the point of shedding your blood. . . . It is for discipline that you have to endure. . . . He disciplines us for our good, that we may share His holiness. For the moment all discipline seems painful rather than pleasant; later it yields the peaceful fruit of righteousness to those who have been trained by it. Therefore lift your drooping hands and strengthen your weak knees and make straight paths for your feet . . . strive for peace with all men, and for the holiness without which no one will see the Lord (Hebr. 12:1-14).

2

The Bible in the Orthodox Church

It is the traditional teaching of the Orthodox Church that the Bible is the scripture of the Church, that it has its proper meaning only within the life and experience of the people of God, that it is not a thing-in-itself which can be isolated from its organic context within the church community, in which and for which and from which it exists. The Bible is the book of the Church. It has no proper standing in itself apart from those who have written it and interpreted it, the people whose vision and action it is meant to inspire and instruct.[1]

Once the Bible has been constituted as the scripture of the Church, it becomes its main written authority, within the Church and not over or apart from it.[2] Everything in the

[1]G. Florovsky, "Sobornost: The Catholicity of the Church," *The Church of God,* ed. Mascall (London, 1934), pp. 62-68; also "Revelation and Interpretation," *Biblical Authority for Today,* ed. Richardson and Schweitzer (London, 1951), pp. 163-164, 170-171, "The Holy Spirit in Revelation," *The Christian East* (Summer, 1932), p. 58 ff., "Scripture and Tradition: An Orthodox Point of View," *Dialogue II* (Minneapolis, 1963), p. 290; S. Verhovskoy, *God and Man* (in Russian; New York, 1956), refs. to unpublished English translation (St. Vladimir's Seminary, New York, 1969), pp. 45-57; N. Arseniev, "The Teaching of the Orthodox Church on the Relation between Scripture and Tradition," *The Eastern Churches Quarterly,* Supplementary Issue, vol. 7 (1947), p. 21; V. Kesich, "Criticism, the Gospel and the Church," *St. Vladimir's Seminary Quarterly* 10 (1966), pp. 155-156; A. Khomiakov, *The Church Is One* (Eastern Orthodox Catholic Church of America, New York, 1953), pp. 22-24.

[2]Cf. A. Khomiakov, "On the Western Confessions of Faith," *Ultimate Questions, An Anthology of Modern Russian Religious Thought,* ed. A. Schmemann (New York, 1965), pp. 50-53. S. Verhovskoy, "The Highest Authority in the Church," *St. Vladimir's Seminary Quarterly* 4 (1960), pp. 76-88; J. Meyendorff, "Historical Relativism and Authority in Christian Dogma," *St. Vladimir's Seminary Quarterly* 11 (1967) pp. 73-86.

Church is judged by the Bible. Nothing in the Church may contradict it. Everything in the Church must be biblical; for the Church, in order to be the Church, must be wholly expressive of the Bible; or more accurately, it must be wholly faithful to and expressive of that reality to which the Bible is itself the scriptural witness.[3]

The Bible lives in the Church. It is an essential element of the organic wholeness of the Church. Without the Church there would be no Bible. The Church has selected and canonized some writings—some and not others—as the true expression of divine revelation, the authentic witness to its divine experience and doctrine.[4] The Church evaluates and interprets those writings which it has chosen, both in a conscious way in expressions of varying degrees of formality and authority and in a more "lived" and unreflecting way in its on-going teaching, worship and life. The Church gives the Bible its life as a book. It provides its existential context, purpose and significance. It makes the book come alive. To isolate the Bible from its vital churchly setting, and to analyse it purely as a thing-in-itself as if its meaning were contained sealed within its covers as a self-enclosed and self-exhaustive phenomenon capable of being fully understood and appreciated directly by anyone in a strictly "worldly" context, would be to violate the book and to make its full significance incapable of being properly and correctly discovered. This is not to say that the Bible is completely and totally useless if read, for example, as "living literature" or even as a "sacred book," and that it cannot speak directly to men who are outside the life of the covenanted people of God. Certainly the Bible

[3]We find a striking similarity between the Bible in the Church and man's situation in the world according to existential phenomenological philosophy. The Bible is always, already discovered in the Church; it is given together with the Church; it cannot be separated from the Church and remain authentically what it is; to put the question about the Bible and the Church is to imply and to affirm in the very asking the existence of the Bible as an element of the Church, together with its meaning and its message. See, *e.g.*, Heidegger's analysis of *Dasein* in the first part of *Being and Time,* trans. J. Macquarrie and E. Robinson (New York, 1962).

[4]For an Orthodox opinion on the biblical canon see W. Schneirla, "The Orthodox Old Testament Canon and the So-called Apocrypha," *St. Vladimir's Seminary Quarterly* 1 (1957), p. 40 ff.; also A. Schmemann, *The Historical Road of Eastern Orthodoxy* (New York, 1963), pp. 42-46.

can be read outside the life of the Church, and certainly it can and it does enlighten and inspire men who are not members of the church family. But even though this happily is the case, it cannot be concluded from this that this is the way the Bible is meant to function in accomplishing that for which it was written. The Bible was compiled by the Church and for the Church. And the Church itself is not understandable without it, both the Church of the Old Testament, with the scriptures of the law and the prophets, and the Church of the New Testament, which fulfills the old and still lives on toward the Kingdom with its own sacred writings at the very center of its doctrine, worship and life.

Revelation and Inspiration

The Orthodox Church has always claimed that the Bible is the Word of God, that it is not merely the product of men or of the Church understood as an exclusively human institution. The Church obviously has realized that although God is the author of the Bible, the book is equally the work of men, of many different men in different times and places. Until now, however, there has been no clearly formulated doctrine of how the Bible is to be understood as being at the same time the Word of God and the word or words of men. The classical formulation of this question in terms of revelation and inspiration arose outside the Orthodox tradition and was imported into Orthodoxy through the westernized schools of recent centuries.[5] One might rightly ask whether these categories have aided or hindered an Orthodox clarification of the problem. It might be more fortunate and fruitful to treat this question from the viewpoint of what the Church has already clearly confessed about the relation of the divine and the human, particularly in reference to creation and salvation, both in terms of christology, from which insights and formulations have also overflowed into the area of ecclesiology, and in terms of the doctrine of man's eternal deification towards God through Christ in the Holy Spirit.

[5] G. Florovsky, *The Ways of Russian Theology* (in Russian; Paris, 1937).

In its deepest spiritual experience and in its clearest doctrinal expressions, as well as in its most living everyday words and actions, the Church presupposes and confesses that God can and does reveal Himself, and that man can and does know Him in His self-revelation. The purpose of man's life is to be in conscious, living, existential communion with God. The whole of creation and the entire Christian dispensation proclaim and bear witness to this eternal goal. St. Gregory of Nyssa, whose theology has inspired much of what is written here, gives us a concise summation of this realization in his *Commentary on the Beatitudes:* "The Lord does not say that it is blessed to know something about God, but to have God present within oneself."[6] Man can know God only by having Him "present within" himself, only by being in living communion with Him. He can know God, as the same saint has put it in another place, only "by being united to Him in purity of life."[7] Man can be in completely self-aware and self-conscious union with God and really know Him—not just something about Him, but God Himself as He is making Himself known.

The revelation of God, the Church teaches, is really of God. It is not of God's essence, which is strictly, ontologically, unknowable. But it is nonetheless really and truly a revelation of God. The classic exposition of this position in the Orthodox Church is well-known.[8] God can be known by men as He reveals Himself in the multitude of His divine manifestations, the uncreated energies, operations, actions, emanations, graces, powers, whatever they be named; which modes of self-revelation are not merely created or contrived entities other than God Himself. Man knows God as He shows Himself and makes Himself known. Man's knowledge is really of God and not merely of some created data or information about Him which, however much it may concern Him and whatever it may be in itself, yields direct knowledge of something other than God Himself.

[6]*Commentary on the Beatitudes* (Ancient Christian Writers 18; Westminster, Maryland, 1954), p. 148.

[7]*Ibid.,* p. 151.

[8]Cf. V. Lossky, *The Mystical Theology of the Eastern Church* (London, 1957). Verhovskoy, *God and Man, passim.*

It is also the undisputed teaching of the Church that every revelation of God is through the Logos in the Holy Spirit.[9] Revelation, whatever its form, is always trinitarian; and so is man's knowing response to that revelation. This doctrine, again clearly if perhaps not that officially formulated, contains within it a doctrine of man. Briefly put, it is that man is the image of God created to know Him and love Him in genuine communion with Him. The union of man with God, which is the way of man's true knowledge of God, requires man's purification from every darkness and sin. It requires man's totally obedient response to the actions which God makes towards him and in him. This knowledge through living communion and union is not intellectual knowledge alone, although the intellect is centrally involved. It is knowledge which involves man's total mental and spiritual and physical purification, primarily rooted and expressed in love.[10]

The knowledge which man has of God through union in truth and purity and love is real knowledge. It is not illusory or arbitrary, relative or subjective in the radical sense that it is imprisoned in the incommunicable interior of a totally isolated and insulated subject. It is mystical knowledge to be sure—religious, spiritual knowledge. But it is objective. It can be reflected upon, spoken about, shared, compared, communicated, discussed, witnessed. It is an objective knowledge which can be criticized and judged, and which in turn can criticize and judge. And yet it is not merely knowledge about something about God, the truth or falsehood of which depends exclusively upon the acceptability of the fundamental data and the logical validity of the subsequent ratiocination but which nevertheless always remains locked within its dialectical, conceptual framework, never touching reality itself. The knowledge of God through direct contact with the divine reality itself is possible, and it is objectively possible for all. This is the very heart of the Christian teaching and life. We will speak more of this below.

According to the Church's doctrine on this same point also—and once more not necessarily formally decreed in this or

[9]*Ibid.*
[10]*Ibid.*

that dogmatic statement but nonetheless universally acknowl-
edged and confessed—man's natural state as image of God
is precisely that dynamic condition in which he possesses the
living knowledge of God through communion in love and
obedience in light and purity of life.[11] Man naturally possesses
this in creation since God reveals Himself and creates in His
Logos and His Spirit, man being the creature who fulfills his
created nature by bearing the Logos-Image and by being
inspired by the divine Spirit. When the human creature de-
forms his divine image and loses his logical character and
quenches the divine breath in himself, then salvific restoration and recreation is required to allow him once more to
fulfill his nature and to live in union with God. The communion which yields knowledge must be re-effected and re-
established. It is a costly process, a redemption. God pays
the price and effects the salvation of His creation in the salvation of His created image. Man is saved from darkness,
the devil and death, and is liberated once more to be in the
dynamic movement of living progression in and toward God
in knowledge of Him. He is set free to be that which he was
created to be, a partaker of the nature of God, a sharer of
the divine life, an appropriator and possessor by grace of
every divine attribute.[12]

In man's darkness and ignorance and blindness and death,
God comes to man as a *revelation*. To know God in this sinful
and blinded condition man requires a special divine *inspiration*. But still it is not at all a "supernatural" revelation and
inspiration. It is not at all as if something completely un-
natural and alien to humanity were being placed upon it from
outside, something literally extra-ordinary and supra-added.
On the contrary. Revelation and inspiration in the dispensation of God, His *oikonomia* in the world, are necessary for

[11]That communion with God is man's natural state, see Lossky, *op. cit.*,
p. 114 ff.; J. Meyendorff, "Orthodox Theology Today," *St. Vladimir's Seminary Quarterly* 13 (1969), p. 82-83; J. Daniélou and H. Musurillo, *From
Glory to Glory, Texts from Gregory of Nyssa's Mystical Writings* (New York,
1961), p. 11.

[12]St. Maximus the Confessor, *The Four Centuries on Charity* 2, 52 (Ancient
Christian Writers 21; New York, 1955), p. 163. 2 Pet. 1:4; 1 Pet. 1:15;
Matt. 5:48.

man in order for him to fulfill his created nature. They are necessary for man in his weakened and corrupted condition, in his ignorance and blindness and death. Revelation in the dispensation, the Judeo-Christian revelation, is a condescension to human weakness, an act of particular kindness and mercy of God, an act of His divine self-emptying so that He could be with man in every possible situation so that there would be no doubt and no excuse left for man. Because man, on account of his sins, can hardly know God in any other way, God comes to him in this special condescending way. He comes as He came in creation, in the same way that He always comes when He comes: through the Logos in the Spirit. In the Old Testament in shadow and in the New Testament in person, God comes to allow knowledge of Himself through communion in purity of life.[13]

The doctrinal formulation of the saving incarnation of the Logos of God can help further in articulating what revelation and inspiration of the Bible can mean, how the Bible can be understood as being both the Word of God and the words of men, both perfectly divine and perfectly human at the same time. Christ is the enfleshed Logos of God, the fulness of divinity bodily, the divine in human form. He is the revelation of God. He is the inspired one. He is the living word. He is the *eikon* in whom man can see God. He is the exegete of God. No man has seen God at any time; the only Son has made Him known.[14]

Christ is the most perfect possible union of God and man, fully divine and fully human, yet one person. The formula about the co-existence and the co-inherence of humanity and divinity in Christ—without separation and without division, yet without confusion and without mixture, the formula of the *Horos* of Chalcedon, which has been accepted and developed by the catholic Church since the fifth century—is the

[13]St. Athanasius in his *On the Incarnation of the Word of God* explicitly teaches that the dispensation and revelation are not special acts of God supra-added to man's nature, but that they are on the contrary condescensions to man's weakness because of his dehumanization and turning away from God (Mowbray, London, 1963), pp. 37-44. See also references to St. John Chrysostom in Kesich, *op. cit.*, p. 154.

[14]*E.g.*, Jn. 1:18, 14:9; Hebr. 1:2; 2 Cor. 3:14, 4:2-4; Gal. 1:6-16; Col. 1:15.

key formulation about how the divine and the human can be
united together and permeate each other and yet each remain
essentially what it is in itself.[15] It affirms that in one concrete
personal act of existence, in one subsistent, concrete existent,
God and man or, more accurately, the divine and the human
can exist with and in the other and penetrate each other so
perfectly and truly that the attributes of one can authentically
be predicated of the other, even though the divine is not
changed by nature into the human nor the human into the
divine. This insight, regardless of how it may be formulated,
is the key insight of the Christian faith into reality itself:
namely, that spiritual realities, even divine and human spiritual
realities, can exist together in the same existent, in the same
concretely-existing entity; that they can co-exist and each
"live in" the other even to the degree that it is perfectly
accurate to say that they are perfectly united and form in a
real way but one organism, with each one at the same time
remaining in itself what it is by nature. Add to this the equally
crucial Christian doctrine that love—and God is love—perfectly
unites on the personal level, thus allowing for the deepest
and most genuine union of persons in interpersonal relationships, and we have the fullest vision into the mystery that
spiritual reality may be at the same time one and many,
perfectly united and yet eternally, essentially distinct; that
many persons can share the same nature, answering with the
same description to the question *what,* and yet each be perfectly unique in his actual existence; that many persons can
be perfectly united not only essentially by nature, being the
same "thing," but that they can be genuinely and truly united
spiritually, existentially in love; that in one person many
levels of reality have the possibility of existing: divine, human,
beastly, demonic; that God can, because of His very divinity,
go out of Himself and descend to the created and the human,
and even, in this condition, enter into servitude, humiliation,
suffering and death; that man, because of his humanity as

[15]For post-Chalcedonian christology in the East see J. Meyendorff, *Christ
in Eastern Christian Thought* (Washington, 1969) and also the very enlightening book by L. Thunberg, *Microcosm and Mediator: The Theological
Anthropology of St. Maximus the Confessor* (Lund, 1965).

created by God can ascend by God's grace to the level of divinity, participating in the nature of God and growing ever more perfectly in divinity, with all of the divine attributes, for eternity. It is within such a vision of reality that all reality must be understood: God and man, the Church and the world, the Kingdom of God. It is within such an understanding also that the Bible may be understood as a phenomenon at the same time fully divine and fully human by the anointing of human words by the Spirit of God, thus making them capable of bearing and of being themselves the divine Word of God.

The christological doctrines of the Church form the paradigm for all of its doctrines about the relationship between the uncreated and the created: in creation itself, in salvation, in deification. The Church affirms in these doctrines that the created is fully open to the uncreated and fully capable of receiving divinity, and that the uncreated is fully open to the created, fully capable of descending and assuming its nature, its flesh and even its death. God can be "all in all"; He can "fill all things with Himself."[16] And in doing this, He can make the human divine, which is man's original and final destiny: to become ever more truly divine in an infinite, eternal progression by participation in divinity.[17] In His divine condescension to humanity and the world, God never ceases to be God. And in his eternal, never-ending ascension to divinity, man never ceases to be man. At each point in these movements, which are in reality two distinct aspects of one and the same spiritual movement, God in His essence remains incomprehensible to creatures, infinitely qualitatively different from the created at each and every stage of His self-emptying coming to the world and of man's self-fulfilling deification in the "realm of God." Indeed the very divinity of God is most fully revealed in the majesty of His humble and loving self-revelation and self-donation to man, just as man's humanity is most genuinely human the greater it appropriates the attributes of divinity, the more man grows closer to God and

[16]Col. 1:9-20, 2:2-3; Eph. 1:9-23, 3:3-10; Liturgy of St. Basil the Great (Orthodox Church in America, New York, 1967), p. 101.

[17]Daniélou, *op. cit.*, pp. 46-71.

realizes the total otherness of Divine Reality.[18]

Given what man has seen, known, experienced and loved in the Church about the interrelations between God and man, it may be possible to formulate how the Church can understand the Bible, how it knows it to be at the same time God's own Word and man's, the product of man as much as of God. The fundamental insight and affirmation must be that theandric existence is possible, that spiritual realities may coexist and in-exist without separation and division in concrete fact, but equally without confusion or mixture as to their nature; that a word may be at the same time perfectly divine and perfectly human without having to admit that true humanity is lost or that the divine, which is supersensual and immaterial in every way, can have sensual and material words.

The Bible is exactly that collection of human writings and human words—and *all* writings and words are human[19]—in which God reveals Himself in human form. The Bible is the divine Word in human scriptural form, fully divine and yet fully human, written in the words of men, filled with the Spirit of God to be the Word of God; the Spirit whose very property it is as a divine person to hide Himself in the human and created and to be always known, when He is known, through His human, created image and agent.[20] So in the Bible the divine Word becomes truly human without ceasing to be divine. And the human words become by the grace of the Spirit the Word of God without ceasing to be human.

It is not necessary, however, in every case to imagine that the writer of a biblical text was fully aware of the implications of his writing, or even aware that his words would one day be seen to be the Word of God, although in the Bible itself it is usually the case that the authors of the texts claim to be expressing God's Word. For it is most directly in their use as vehicles for knowledge of and communion with God, when they come alive in the Church in the Spirit, when they

[18]Thunberg, *op. cit.,* p. 33; N. Arseniev, *Revelation of Life Eternal* (St. Vladimir's Seminary, New York, n. d.), pp. 89-90.

[19]Kesich, *op. cit.* Cf. Gregory of Nyssa's thought on the meaning of words in his *Answer to Eunomius' Second Book* (Nicene and Post Nicene Fathers, Second Series, vol. 5, pp. 272-281).

[20]Lossky, *op. cit.,* pp. 166-170.

open the divine reality to man in the Spirit, that the scriptures reveal themselves and fulfill themselves as God's Word. Who can, in any case, really know what was in the mind and the heart of the writers of texts which came to be parts of the Bible? Who can know or discover by any means and method what was their personal purpose or intention in writing what they have written? Or what God Himself had in mind at the time of the writing? But in the vision of God which the Bible yields in the Church, within the context particularly of the fulfilled Church of the New Testament, in which nothing is lacking of the divine fulness and in which the most perfect possibilities exist for ever-more-perfect penetration into divine wisdom—in this reality in which the Bible lives, there is nothing hypothetical and imaginary, nothing arbitrary or tentative. And it is this real experience which is the ground of the conviction that the Bible is indeed God's Word in human form, and not any theory about how the texts were produced. For the Church has proclaimed the scriptures to be inspired only after examining the fruit which the scriptures yield, the communion and knowledge of God which the scriptures make possible in the life of the Church, understood as life in union with God through Christ, the divine Word enfleshed, in the Holy Spirit.[21]

The Bible is therefore a divine-human reality by being "of the Church," which by every traditional Christian definition, intuition and experience is a mystery like that of the person of Christ Himself; or more exactly, an element of the mystery of Christ Himself, the whole Christ, head and body.[22] The Old Testament scriptures are an element of the mystery of Christ by their incorporation into the Church, by their

[21]The argument from the experience of the Church is typical of traditional theology. In this way Ignatius of Antioch argued for the reality of the flesh and suffering of Christ (Trallians 10-11:1); Athanasius for the divinity of the Logos (*On the Incarnation*, pp. 88-95); Gregory of Nazianzus for the divinity of the Holy Spirit (*Fourth Theological Oration*, Nicene and Post-Nicene Fathers, Second Series, vol. 7, p. 326 ff.); Cyril of Alexandria for the title of Theotokos for the Virgin Mary (Anathema XI against Nestorius, Nicene and Post Nicene Fathers, Second Series, vol. 14, p. 217). And in this way the Church confirmed the inspiration of the scriptures and selected the canonical books. See Schmemann, n. 4 *supra*.

[22]Kesich, *op. cit.*, p. 152.

completed and fulfilled understanding in the new and everlasting covenant. And the scriptures of the New Testament
are themselves the product of the mystery of Christ, the
scriptural witness to the completed and fulfilled events and
life in Him. In this perspective, the ways of studying and
interpreting the Old and the New Testament scriptures necessarily differ. On the altars of the Church, as a symbolic
example of this, it is just the four gospels which are en-
throned, and not the entire Bible. There is a distinction made
by the Church itself as to the relative place and importance of
the various biblical books. The distinctions in the historical
determination of the canon is further evidence of this. But
nevertheless, once it is constituted and evaluated within the
Church, the entire Bible remains—even with the full recognition of the varying importance and value of its books in relation to the fulness of the mystery of Christ—totally a theandric, divine-human phenomenon: the product of divine and
human collaboration and cooperation both in its writing and
in its understanding.[23] The Bible is wholly the Word of God
and the word of man, one Word. And this is affirmed and
confessed not on the basis of speculative theories about its
production, but primarily on the basis of its existence and use
within the community of those who through Christ and the
Spirit are, by means of it, being united to God.

The Bible and Knowledge

As a manifestation of God, the deepest meaning of the
Bible lies not merely in what it tells about God, but in how
it yields true knowledge of God by bringing man into living
communion with Him. In the Church the Bible exists as a
vehicle of man's union and knowledge of divine reality and
of all reality in God. The Bible can be called a symbolic book
in the literal sense that it brings together into union the divine
and the human. It can be called a mystical book in the sense

[23]Athanasius, *On the Incarnation*, pp. 39-41. Thunberg, in reference to St.
Maximus the Confessor, *op. cit.* pp. 82-83. On the cooperation between God
and man, the doctrine of synergy, see Lossky, *op. cit.*, p. 185 ff.

that it participates in the mystery of Christ, the mystery which is Christ and the Church, indeed the mystery of all that exists. Within this mystery, the Bible is the logical instrument which unites God and man on the level of *word*, which in the tradition of both the Bible and the Church of old and new covenants does not imply mere information or communication of data, but revelation and presence of the subject himself.[24] In the biblical tradition God is present in and through His Word; He is identified with it. One who is in contact with His Word is in contact with Him. It is the same with man. The word is a self-manifestation, a revelation, a presence, a power, a mode of communion and union between hearer and speaker. And yet it has in itself also a certain subsistence of its own, a sort of self-independence once pronounced which allows it all the more to be that which it is and to perform its function.

The word makes possible a living relationship with its subject and so makes possible what the churchly, biblical tradition has always understood by *knowledge*, namely the conscious awareness of being in a living relationship and existentially concrete communion with the object known; a state or action which requires for its integrity spiritual qualities in the knower other than those of a purely mental character, and also an ontological correlation between the knower and the object known.[25] In relation to God, man can truly know God because he is created in His image and likeness to hear His Word and to live and to know by His Spirit. Thus there is an essential "built-in" condition in man, built in by God Himself, which allows man truly to know God and to fulfill his existence through this very knowledge.

But there is also an existential condition necessary for man to know God. Man must be true to his nature. He must personally and freely will to be what he is created to be, and to

[24]See the references to the meaning of *Word* in P. Grelot, *The Bible, Word of God* (New York, 1968), p. 6; R. Latourelle, *Theology of Revelation* (New York, 1968), p. 29 ff.

[25]L. Bouyer, *The Spirituality of the New Testament and the Fathers* (New York, 1960), pp. 15 ff., 182 ff., 211-275. Note also how central is the gnostic element in the revelation theology of the church fathers, as shown in Latourelle, *op. cit.*, pp. 87-132.

do that for which he was made, to progress and develop
eternally in union with God and all things in Him, ever
more perfectly acquiring the full spectrum of divine characteristics: life, truth, wisdom, goodness, holiness, purity, beauty,
joy . . . and especially love. To know God, therefore, man
must actively retain and develop his nature as the divine
image and likeness.[26] An image perverted, deformed, distorted,
void of divine light, developing in darkness and blindness
due to sin, cannot possibly know God, who is the archetype
of all that is living, true and good. Thus there is the existential
condition of moral and spiritual rectitude which is an absolutely necessary prerequisite for knowledge. Without this
condition and spiritual attitude—purity, honesty, openness,
detachment—there is no chance for real knowledge. The Bible
itself bears witness to this as does the Jesus presented on its
pages, who, in the prophetic tradition, accuses the ignorant
not merely of a lack of facts or proper information or education or mental ability, but of voluntary foolishness, blindness
and sin. In the biblical and churchly perspective, the man
ignorant of God is willfully so for evil reasons. He refuses
to understand. He is a fool who loves darkness more than
light. He has betrayed his human nature and task. Without
such a view of man's knowing function and possibiilties, it is
impossible to understand not only the prophets of the Old
Testament and the fathers of the Church, but also Jesus Himself.

To return to our present concern at this point, we repeat
that it is the witness of the Church that the whole Bible reveals God and makes Him known in His Word; that in and
through the Bible—as it lives in the community of God's
people through Christ, the enfleshed Word, and through the
Spirit—man can come to genuine knowledge of God Himself
in communion with Him. In this perspective, the final meaning of the Bible, therefore, is seen not to lie within it as a
text or a collection of texts. Its final significance and purpose
lies in reality itself, the reality to which it itself bears witness,

[26]Athanasius, op. cit., p. 38; Gregory of Nyssa, in Daniélou, From Glory
to Glory, pp. 10 ff, 100-102, 110-114; Maximus the Confessor, and the analysis
of image of God in Greek patristics, Thunberg, op. cit., pp. 120-139.

the reality of God and all things in Him. The purpose of the Bible is to reveal God, to point beyond itself to Him, to indicate Him, to disclose Him, to lead man into living communion with Him, to lead man into true knowledge. Through the Bible man should see, hear, taste and even touch the Word of Life, who is God Himself, the ground and the goal of all that exists.[27]

St. Gregory of Nyssa, to use his words again, put this crucial point this way in two separate works:

> ... the Prophets, the Evangelists, and the Apostles. ... all of them have become rivers for us, drawing their waters so far as they could from dark, hidden and invisible treasuries. Even though everyone of these is full to overflowing with the vastness and depth of doctrine, yet they are merely *drops* of dew in comparison with actual Truth.[28]

> I have heard the divinely inspired Scriptures disclose marvelous things about the transcendent Nature—yet what are they when compared to the Nature Itself? For even if I were capable of grasping all that the Scripture says, yet that which is signified is more. ... So it is with the words said about God in Holy Scripture, which are expounded to us by men inspired by the Holy Spirit. If measured by our understanding, they are indeed exalted above all greatness; yet they do not reach the majesty of truth. ... what are they compared with the reality?[29]

The Bible is not depreciated by the saint nor by the Church, which holds both the Bible and such an appreciation of it with greatest reverence. On the contrary. The reality is far greater than all that the Bible can express. Yet the Bible signifies again, in various ways and in various degress of

---

[27]Jn. 1:1-5; 1 Jn. 1:1-4; Florovsky, "Scripture and Tradition: An Orthodox Point of View," p. 293.

[28]*Commentary on the Canticle of Canticles,* in Daniélou, *From Glory to Glory,* p. 249.

[29]*On the Beatitudes, edit. cit.,* p. 155-156.

completion, exactly this reality. It is through the Bible that this reality is reached. It is by means of the Bible living in the Church that this reality is revealed, experienced and known.

The knowledge which the Bible makes possible in the Church is real knowledge. It can be checked as all knowledge can be checked, only in reference to the object of knowledge itself, only by living verification through contact and personal experience. A book about atoms, for example, can only be evaluated when one is in contact with real atoms. Without such an experience, texts about atoms may be trusted or distrusted, believed or doubted, but nothing more. Knowledge comes exclusively by way of direct experience. Only in the light of such experience can any words about the object in question be tested and judged.

Any text which claims to treat reality, even spiritual reality or divine reality, is used in two ways as far as knowledge is concerned. On the one hand the text can enlighten reality. It can introduce people to it, create the desire in men to know it, make some descriptions and explanations of it, theorize about it in relation to its properties and possibilities, its relations to other realities, *etc.* It can allow men to recognize it when they actually meet it in reality. On the other hand, the reality itself can enlighten the text written about it. It can allow the text to be evaluated and judged as to its truth, as to its worth, as to the accuracy and adequacy and meaning of its concepts, images, words, symbols, logical development, *etc.* In texts dealing with spiritual reality, because of the nature of such reality, the object in question may be met directly in and through the text itself. This is particularly the case in books dealing, *e.g.*, with artistic, poetic, philosophical and religious subjects, as well as in texts in which the author has the express purpose of revealing himself and his own ideas and opinions. But in each and every case, the words of books are never ends in themselves. They inevitably point beyond themselves as words to realities. Stopping at the level of words, one never comes to knowledge.

The Bible may be trusted. But perhaps the arguments to do so on the strictly human level are not much more convincing than those which would say that the book should be doubted. In any case, the point here is that trust is not enough. This is a message of the Bible itself. Man is created to know. And the Bible yields knowledge.[30]

Man must come into living contact and communion with the reality about which the Bible speaks and to which it bears witness. Man must come to have for himself the knowledge of the truth, to know God and Jesus Christ whom He has sent, which, according to the scriptures, is eternal life.[31] This knowledge is possible. Within the Church the Bible makes it possible. For as a text about atoms or about love only yields knowledge when one contacts through it the real atom or experiences love; and as the same text can only be judged scientifically on the basis of the knowledge of the reality itself according to the manner in which the object of knowledge makes itself known in actuality; so also the Bible has meaning only as it enlightens divine reality, discloses it to man and leads him into communion with it; and so too can the Bible be judged and criticized only in reference to the knowledge of the reality which it claims to disclose, and only in the way in which it claims to do so, namely in the mystical life of the Christian Church. Thus the Bible may be accepted or rejected, denied or affirmed only on the basis of one's experience (or lack of it) of God and of all things in Him within the Church, of which the Bible is an integral element and which claims to yield experience of that whereof the Bible speaks.

The Bible in the Church

The Church is not to be understood here as a human institution, an organization among many human organizations. It is to be understood as the theandric life of progressive union with God through Christ, the incarnate divine Logos, in the Holy Spirit. In its sacramental-spiritual life, the Church is exactly this. It is for this reason only that everything in the Church exists—including the Bible. In this sense the Church

[30]See n. 26 *supra.*
[31]Jn. 17:3.

is not opposed to the world of God's creation. It is opposed
to the world of sinful passions and death, however, which
is not the natural world of God's creation.[32] The Church is
the world—the world as God created it to be and the world
as God has saved it to be. In the Church the possibility is
given to see and to know and to live as man must naturally
live: in communion with God, all men and the entire cosmos,
through Christ in the Holy Spirit.[33]

It is important to see right now that there is a trinitarian
foundation to all of reality. The world is created by God
through His Word in His Spirit. Man is the image of God by
bearing the Word-Image and by being the vessel and temple
of the Spirit. The dispensation of salvation is effected through
the Word and the Spirit, both in the Old Testament and in
the New, albeit, obviously, in radically different ways. Christ
Himself is the Word of God who bears the Spirit. The Church
is the body of the enfleshed Word, filled with the Spirit. The
Kingdom of God, of which the Church already now is the
mystical image and presence in the old world, is the fulness
of creation filled with the Word, governed and enlightened
by Him, united to God through Him for eternity, once more
in the Spirit who fills all things.

The Church as the experience already now of eternal life
is in all of its essential aspects strictly trinitarian. The inaugu-
ration into the Church, for example, is by death and resurrection in Christ (baptism) and sealing with "the seal of the
gift of the Holy Spirit" (chrismation-confirmation). The order
of the Church exists to make God present through Christ,
in every aspect of His messianic presence and power: savior,
priest, victim, lamb, teacher, pastor, healer, forgiver, servant,
etc., once again by the Holy Spirit. Marriage is an image of
God and Israel, Christ and the Church, the Kingdom of God
through Christ in the Spirit. Everything which is authentically
of the Church is trinitarian in its essence and existence, in its
content and life. And the Bible is no exception. It is the
scriptural Word of God inspired by the Holy Spirit not only

[32]St. Isaac of Syria, "Directions on Spiritual Training," nos. 22, 25, 26,
269, in *Early Fathers from the Philokalia,* trans. Kadloubovsky and Palmer
(London, 1954), pp. 187, 188, 272.
    [33]A. Schmemann, *Sacraments and Orthodoxy* (New York, 1965).

in its writing, composition, collection of texts and canon-
ization, but also in its interpretation and use in the Church
as a vehicle toward the experience of that very reality which
it reveals and to which it bears witness.

It is important to see the trinitarian foundation of all
things, not merely to see that each is ontologically connected
with the other, but to see as well how Christ is indeed the
center of all things: creation, man, the world, history, the
Church, the Kingdom . . . and the Bible. The Bible itself
declares this.[34]

Christ is the historical, scriptural and spiritual center of
the Bible. This was always the expressed understanding of
the catholic Christian Church. The Old Testament is fulfilled
in the New and finds its true meaning in it. The New Testament lies hidden in the Old and finds its foreshadowing in
it.[35] Christ is the center and unifier of both testaments. He is
the origin and end of scriptures, as He is the origin and end
of all creation.[36] He is the Word incarnate, present in the
scriptures as He is incarnate in the world.[37] He is the fulfillment of the law and the prophets.[38] He is the Head of the
Church, through whom the Holy Spirit comes upon all flesh,
inspiring and enlightening those who receive Him from God
by Christ so that they might "know all things."[39] Thus the
Old Testamental scriptures are understandable in their fulness only in the light of the New. And the scriptures of the
New Testament are themselves understandable in their fulness only in the light of Christ in the Spirit of Truth in the
Church.[40]

The Church is the experience of the messianic age, in
which, according to the scriptures, all men are "taught of

---

[34]Jn. 1:1-18, 5:46; Acts 7:1-53; Col. 1:15-19; Eph. 1:20-23; Phil. 2:9-11;
et al.

[35]H. DeLubac, *The Sources of Revelation* (New York, 1968), pp. 80-81;
Florovsky, "Revelation and Interpretation," p. 168.

[36]DeLubac, *ibid.*, p. 100 ff.

[37]Thunberg, *op. cit.*, p. 82, 150.

[38]Matt. 5:17, 16:10; Lk. 16:16; DeLubac, *op. cit.*, p. 100 ff.

[39]Jn. 2:20.

[40]DeLubac, *op. cit.*; cf. Florovsky, "The Holy Spirit in Revelation." Lk.
24:44-46; Jn. 14:26.

God.''[41] It is the age of the final, everlasting covenant, which
has no tablets of stone but whose law is the law of the Holy
Spirit written on the tablets of human hearts.[42] It is the time
of the manifestation and indwelling in men of God Himself.
The Church, understanding and experiencing itself this way,
has understood and experienced the written words of the
Bible also in this context. Christ remains forever the Master
and Teacher, forever making God known in the Spirit, forever opening the scriptures to His disciples, showing how
Moses, the psalms and the prophets have spoken of Him
so that the disciples themselves might "show from the scriptures" that reality is indeed this way.[43] Thus the Bible is read
in the Church in the perspective of fulfillment.

The texts of the New Testament were consciously written
with this in mind, and in the Church's liturgy they are
used exactly in this way. The time of the Church is the time
of the outpouring of the Spirit on all flesh.[44] To fall back
from this condition of salvation and to compromise it in any
way, either by lack of faith or by a false biblicism—whether
of fundamentalist or criticalist variety—is to fall back from
the fulness of life given by God through Christ and the
Spirit in the Church and to deny the reality of that which the
Bible itself declares. It is indeed to fall back to a sub-human
level of existence, far below man's original dignity and
destiny in creation.

Spiritual Exegesis

The way of interpreting and understanding the Bible in
the context of the Church may be called spiritual exegesis—
exegesis in the Holy Spirit. It may also simply be called
Christian exegesis or churchly exegesis.[45] Exegesis in the Holy
Spirit, in the context of fulfillment, is the only method of
exegesis which the Church has for its Bible. The Church uses

[41]Jer. 31:34; Is. 54:13; Jn. 6:45.
[42]2 Cor. 3:3; Jer. 31:33.
[43]Matt. 23:10; Lk. 24:32, 44-45; Acts 18:28.
[44]Acts 2:17 ff.
[45]DeLubac, op. cit.; Florovsky, "Revelation and Interpretation," p. 170.

the Bible exclusively in this way in its total life: theologically, doctrinally, liturgically, spiritually, homiletically. There are various types of spiritual exegesis, formed by various aspects of the Church's life and experience. Before even briefly discussing these forms of biblical exegesis, however, it is necessary to make some comments about the opinion that spiritual exegesis is uncritical and unscientific, without authoritative criteria of operation and conclusion; that it makes the Bible a mere "book of riddles," the understanding of which is "doomed to failure" because it opens the way for "unlimited fantasy."[46]

In the first place we find it necessary to repeat what we said above, that the Church's tradition would hardly be ready to admit that the knowledge of God in Christ and the Spirit is not real knowledge or real truth. The entire theology of the Church, its anthropology and soteriology, its ecclesiology and eschatology are based exactly on this premise: God has revealed Himself and men can know Him in His revelation. Man knows God, not just some things about Him, not even some specially revealed information, but God Himself. To deny this is to deny the Bible and the Church and the reality which they make known.

In addition, the Church at no time has opposed faith and mystery to knowledge. It has always claimed that everything must be kept together, that divine mysteries are revealed and that man can know them and believe in them, knowing what he believes and believing what he knows, and growing in both. In this age faith may be central and knowledge "in part"; but this knowledge is still knowledge, knowledge of the divine reality and not merely of words or concepts about it. The Church has never admitted that knowledge properly so called is limited to things measurable and weighable. It has claimed that the knowledge of God, beyond matter, space and time, is possible; that this knowledge is indeed man's highest glory, begun already in the space and time of the old world within the context of the new world which is made present in mystery in the Church.

[46]N. Ozerov, "On Biblical Interpretation," *St. Vladimir's Seminary Quarterly* 3 (1959), p. 28.

Furthermore, the Church would not say that the knowledge of God, and of spiritual reality generally, is subjective, illusory, whimsical, capricious, the product of fantasy. It would say that it is objective in the sense that it is real and that all men can have contact with the same reality. It would claim, further, that such reality may be known exactly as all reality is known: by actual contact and experience, within the conditions and context of its self-revelation. These are the principles and conditions of all knowledge which is truly scientific. They require, as we have mentioned above, openness on the part of the knower, the unprejudiced willingness to enter into communion with the object of knowledge on its own terms, and not according to criteria established by the knower apart from the "claims" of the object itself.

It is our opinion that churchly exegesis of the Bible wishes to operate according to such objective principles. In the first place, this manner of interpreting the Bible respects both the text and the context of scripture. It deals with what the text actually says, understood as an organic whole, with full consideration of the proper place and value of each particular part within the whole. It deals with the text as given and affirmed by the community which has written and adopted it, neither picking and choosing texts nor determining texts on the basis of criteria other than those which are born of the life and experience of the churchly community. It incorporates into its method of interpretation not only the factors of progressive historical development, especially in relation to the Old Testament, and of the form and content of the words and images used in the texts, but also the fact that the interpretation is undertaken within the context of the existential fulfillment of the scriptures in the New Testament Church, in which Christ has come and the Holy Spirit is given. In operating this way, this method of interpretation ultimately uses the texts as all texts should be used in relation to knowledge: it passes beyond the written data and information to the reality about which it speaks and to which it itself bears witness. To use the Bible in any other way and to determine criteria and principles for its interpretation with the pretension of gaining its true and genuine meaning is to be dishonest to the Bible itself as well as to the community in which it is discovered and in which it discloses itself. Such an attempt at establishing criteria of biblical interpretation would be subjective and unscientific. For although one may doubt what the Bible claims about itself and about divine-human reality, and one may further question the claims of the people who have produced the texts and their further evaluation and use of them, one can hardly doubt that an objective study and interpretation of these texts must necessarily consider these things in order to be truly objective and scientific.

It is possible that the spiritual method of interpreting the Bible in the Church can be accused of being totally uninterested in historical, literary, philological, cultural, archeological and other such studies made concerning the Bible. And with justification one could affirm in relation to the scriptures what has been affirmed in a quite different area: that "to argue that some phenomena transcend precise measurement . . . is no excuse for neglecting the arduous task of carefully analysing what *can* be measured."[47] In biblical studies there is certainly much that *can* be measured and at present as at no time previously there are precision instruments for measuring. But once again, it would be plainly incorrect to contend that the Church of both the old and the new covenants was completely uninterested in measuring the measurable in the Bible. The fact that the questions in times past were different ones than many of us have today, the fact that there was a lack of sufficient scholarly information, the fact that there was a different appreciation of history, particularly in the patristic period, and a definite tendency to idealize and spiritualize all reality—all of these factors and many others obviously allow us to have many criticisms and reservations about the fruits of biblical exegesis in times past. But these factors do not allow us to conclude that the interpreters of scripture were uninter-

[47]J. J. Servan-Schreiber, *The American Challenge* (New York, 1969), p. 80. See also Ozerov, *op. cit.;* Kesich, *op. cit.;* and T. Stylianopoulos, "Historical Studies and Orthodox Theology," *The Greek Orthodox Theological Review* 12 (1967), pp. 394-419. These are Orthodox opinions relative to historical criticism and the Bible. See also on the point of history the remarks of Grelot, *op. cit.,* pp. 115-124.

ested in the biblical texts as texts, and were unwilling to use whatever methods were available to them to understand the meaning of the words.

History shows us that the churchly interpreters of scripture were always studying the texts as texts. They did so to the measure that they were able, and also to the extent that they considered such studies fruitful and necessary.[48] Even such notorious spiritualizers as Origen and St. Gregory of Nyssa were meticulously interested in the text of the Bible.[49] They had the sincere desire to interpret the text of scripture, to discover and lay bare its meaning and message and not one of their own creation. They studied texts, compared and contrasted them, trying sincerely to discover the most authentic versions. They studied words passionately, trying to find their true meaning in context, both specifically in the given passage as well as generally in the whole Bible and life of the Church. They did work in philology and etymology—one may question how successfully, but one cannot deny that they tried and considered it important. They even attempted certain formal studies to gain more complete understanding.[50] Here again, although the success can be questioned, the attempt must be recognized, and it must be admitted that the traditional commentators on scripture did not consider such things as entirely irrelevant and useless to their task of understanding and expounding God's Word.

Concerning this method of exegesis—the interpretation of the Bible in Christ, in the Spirit, in the Church—it must be admitted also that those who were commenting on the Bible engaged in what we today would call critical studies to the

[48]Cf. John Chrysostom, *Homilies on St. John,* homily 2.

[49]In regard to Origen, see Daniélou, *Origen* (New York, 1955), pp. 133-138. It should never be forgotten that for all of its importance and influence, Origen's biblical exegesis was not accepted by the Church. For Gregory of Nyssa, his interest in the text as text can be seen in his treatises *On the Life of Moses* and *Commentary on the Canticle of Canticles.* See also his *Answer to Eunomius' Second Book,* pp. 276, 294, 308; and *On the Soul and the Resurrection* (same translation), p. 439.

[50]On this basis Origen rejects the Pauline authorship of Hebrews. Daniélou, *Origen,* p. 138. It is interesting to see Chrysostom in his commentary on Hebrews, from intrinsic evidence as he sees it, accepting the authorship of Paul.

extent that they considered such studies as truly relevant to the Bible, enlightening and fruitful for the discovery of its divine, eternal meaning within the life of the final, everlasting covenant of the New Testament Church. This is what they were after: the meaning of the Bible for the Christian people, the meaning of the Bible for those who in Christ and the Spirit already are themselves the living dwelling-place of God. They wanted to understand the texts in the light of divine eternity. For them this was the true and genuine meaning of scripture, the way to the real knowledge of God Himself and of all things in Him, by way of living experience.

At the present time Christians are blessed with virtually limitless resources for illumining biblical history and biblical texts. The mistake would be to think that the complete understanding of the Bible and the fullest knowledge of divine revelation can be attained by the use of these resources alone, by some authoritative and perfectly objective criteria discoverable and practicable on an exclusively human, however scholarly, level. For, in the tradition of the Church, what the Bible really says has never been considered to be discoverable by historical, philological, cultural studies alone. What the Bible really says is what it says to the Church, in the Church, in the trinitarian context of the "last times."[51] Certain technical studies of the type mentioned above are absolutely necessary in allowing the Church to understand its scripture and to fulfill itself as life in union with God. But some such studies which have been presented as of the greatest importance and significance for understanding the Bible are in fact plainly irrelevant to this end, and others have gone beyond their limits as bases of interpretation, since their conclusions can be nothing more than hypotheses.[52]

[51]DeLubac, *op. cit.*, p. 151 ff; Florovsky, "The Holy Spirit in Revelation," p. 55 ff; Kesich, *op. cit.*

[52]All studies which enlighten the text of the Bible are critically necessary inasmuch as they allow for the fuller and deeper understanding of the Bible in the Church. It would be incorrect to imagine, however, that such studies taken in themselves can produce the meaning of scripture. It would be equally incorrect in our opinion to think that such studies can be done without the perspective of churchly life and experience; for there is no study and no knowledge received in a vacuum without presuppositions, attitudes, interests, questions, *etc.* brought from the side of the subject which determine to a large

There is another point which should again be stressed
before we pass to a brief discussion of the types of churchly-
spiritual exegesis. Because of the Christian appreciation of
the nature of man, the nature of the Church and the nature of
God, it has always been understood and defended that the
knowledge of spiritual things is not only possible, but that it
is the knowledge most proper to man, the deepest knowledge
possible for the creature made in the image of God for union
with Him. In this sense the knowledge of spiritual and divine
reality is objective knowledge, since it is open to and indeed
required of everyone.

If men are really created in the image and likeness of
God; if they all really do share an identical humanity, an
identical human nature and condition; and if it is indeed the
same God who is the archetype of every man as well as His
creator and savior, the one in whose communion and knowledge man fulfills his very humanity; and if finally it is the
same Word-Christ and same Spirit involved with everyone
and everything; then it can only be concluded—as in fact the
Church concludes—that the experience and knowledge of all
this is the same for all, that it is objective and concrete, that
truth is really one and the same for everyone.

Reality has many faces, to be sure; and different perspec-
tives on the same reality are not only due to the limited positions and situations of men. God Himself, the Ultimate
Reality, is infinite in the ways in which He reveals Himself

extent the results of the investigation. The context of even the most formal
studies of the Bible should not be one or another theory of knowledge, language, literature, history, philosophy, but the living life and faith of the Church
concretely expressed in its theology, liturgy, spirituality, canons, councils, and
in the Bible itself.

An example of an interesting but in the final analysis irrelevant study of
the Bible relative to its exegesis is, for instance, that of biblical authorship.
The meaning of Isaiah 53, or the Letter to the Hebrews, is the same for the
Church no matter who wrote the texts.

Another example of futile study as far as the understanding of the Bible
is concerned is that of attempting to find the exact mind and intention of the
hagiographer. How can this ever be known for certain? And even if it could
be known, what effect would such knowledge have on the meaning of the
given text in the context of the fulfilled life of the Christian Church? It must
be said also that in every case historical investigation is hypothetical by its
very nature. Relative to the Bible, it may certainly enlighten, but it never
conclusively determines.

and so also in the ways in which He is known by men. The diversity of knowledge, therefore, comes not merely from the side of men. It comes also from the side of God, from the side of reality itself, from the Divine Being or Supra-Being, the aspects of whose self-revelations, operations and energies are literally numberless, and whose essence is literally inexhaustible and incomprehensible to creatures.[53] But even for all of its many-sidedness and multiformity, spiritual reality is still knowable to men. It is not illusory, vague or subjective. It is, on the contrary, the most concrete and objective knowledge, because it is the most real. It is the ground of all other knowledge, lower forms of knowledge, we might say—those further removed from Ultimate Reality, those involving more mediate, indirect means of cognition. It has always been the biblical-churchly teaching (as well as that of certain philosophies outside the realm of this influence) that God is the source of all wisdom and knowledge, and that all things can be known in Him, or that when all things are fully known, they are seen to be grounded in Him. It is the biblical-Christian teaching in addition (and once again some other religious and philosophical schools would not be excluded) that man by direct, immediate intuition can know this Ultimate Reality,[54] the one who reveals Himself in a multitude of ways and forms, the unchangeable source under every change, both divine and human, if we may dare to put it so; and that man does so by passing beyond himself, and certainly beyond the rational methods of cognition involving concepts and words and syllogistic ratiocination by which God cannot be known, to the intuitive, visionary knowledge by which God is known. As the ground of all logic, God cannot be known by logic. His existence may be inferred, but He is not yet known.[55] He is known by spiritual intuition which is not, as some say, irrational, but which is, according to the Church's tradition, the highest form of human rationality, a use of the mind (of course not disconnected from goodness and love) which pene-

[53]Cf. Gregory of Nyssa, *Commentary on the Canticle of Canticles,* trans. Daniélou, *From Glory to Glory,* pp. 245-246.

[54]*Ibid.,* p. 242.

[55]Gregory of Nazianzus, *Second Theological Oration,* p. 290. Gregory of Nyssa, *On the Beatitudes,* pp. 99-100.

trates the very depths of divinity, becoming itself divine in communion with God Himself.[56] When man has this form of knowledge, he has the most genuine knowledge possible to men, the knowledge which is the basis for all other forms of conceptual knowledge, the most real science which is the basis for all of the human and natural (in the everyday use of these words) sciences.[57] This highest science is communicable and discussable. If words are not adequate to it, there are words about it, even words of negative, apophatic character in which communication in relation to it can be carried on, particularly among those who have the same experience. It is possible also that one with such knowledge can preach about it and teach about it and bear witness to it and recognize it in others, *etc.* It is not blind and irrational nor radically, ontologically subjective. It is the knowledge to which all men are called who are called to be saved and to come to the knowledge of the truth.

Such knowledge can be attained, as we have already repeated over and again, only according to its own nature and manner of revealing itself and being attained by men,

[56]There is the tendency to think that traditional churchly gnosiology is either detached intellectualism or irrational mysticism. What must be seen is that the *mind* is certainly central, but it is not detached from other qualities, particularly love. It is precisely when the mind and heart are united, and when man is fully integrated, with each element of his being purified and humanized, that he is capable of knowing God, by way of the divine manifestation in the divine energies. In a word, the mind is central but not in a purely intellectualistic way such as in the case of non-Christian gnosticism, or Origenism or Eunomianism, or in the type of gnosiology and theology which would say that any person with the correct data and the correctly functioning logical apparatus can know God or what there is to be known about him. The mind is central for gnosis, but true gnosis achieves itself particularly in relation to God when united with, and even in a sense being transformed into, love. Cf. Lossky, *The Vision of God,* pp. 24-26, 66-74, 108-110, 136-137.

[57]The intuition of the Absolute is the basis of all logical systems and makes them possible and meaningful; thus Verhovskoy, *God and Man,* pp. 11-19. It is our opinion also that this is what Anselm of Canterbury was getting at with his famous "ontological argument." It was not the case of a dialectical discovery, but the intuition of the Reality which is the ground of dialectics and makes true reasoning possible. Of course this Absolute, the Reality, must be alive, personal, eternal, spiritual. And the knowledge of this Reality is given in revelation not as in opposition to reason, or as supernatural, but as allowing man to be most human and to use his mind as fully and perfectly as possible.

only according to its own particular spiritual conditions. The prime condition for such divine knowledge is the condition of purity. This is the universal teaching of the Bible and the Church's tradition. And it applies even in relation to the exegesis of the Bible. The patristic texts are literally full of warnings that without purity the scriptures cannot be known, particularly the purification which is given in Christ and the Spirit.[58] We have referred to this above, and we refer to it again in this context of spiritual exegesis: those who deform the truth are guilty of folly and sin. This obviously does not refer to those who have been classically described as the involuntarily ignorant, those who fail to see and to believe because of lack of witness or the scandal of those who claim to know, but it applies directly to members of the household who fail to see the truth because of personal choice (heresy in the literal sense means *choice*) and because of the impurity of their cognitive vision due to sin. Only in such a perspective can we understand the ferocity of the prophets, the fathers and the Lord Himself.

Types of Spiritual Exegesis

Spiritual exegesis of the Bible was the method used in the Church universally in its first millenium of existence in both East and West. In this period there is not only a remarkable agreement on the way of understanding and using the Bible in the Church, but a striking agreement in actual interpretations and usages as well.[59] Right here we must mention, however, that methodology alone does not guarantee the same conclusions. It is not right to ask why, if the methodology of

[58]Gregory of Nyssa, *Commentary on the Canticle of Canticles*, pp. 152-153; Gregory Nazianzus, *Theological Orations* I and II, pp. 285, 288, 289; Athanasius, *On the Incarnation*, p. 96; John Chrysostom, *Homilies on St. John*, pp. 2, 3. It must be noticed that purification does not merely apply to spirituality. It means also the sacramental experience of faith, the putting on of Christ and communion with Him in the Church.

[59]Cf. DeLubac, *op. cit.*; Daniélou, *From Shadows to Reality* (London, 1960); Daniélou, *The Bible and the Liturgy* (Notre Dame, 1961). Although Daniélou deals with the Eastern Church tradition, a work in this tradition similar to DeLubac would be most welcome.

the first centuries was generally the same, the exegetical conclusions were not equally so, thus implying that there should
be no heresies, no splits in the Church, no divergencies in the
understanding of the texts of the scripture.

In the first place there were exegetical methods which
were not of the Church and consequently not in the Church
(*e.g.,* gnostic understandings of the Bible and the Christian
faith). But also within the Church, even with a fundamental
unity in methodology (and we would include Alexandria and
Antioch within this fundamental unity,[60] for both schools
were "spiritual" in our use of term) there were incorrect
usages of the method, poor or extreme usages which did not
depend on the method as such but on its implementation. For
whatever method is used, even the methods with the most
clearly expressed and agreed upon criteria of judgment, there
is never an automatic arrival at the same conclusions. Two
scientists using the same method can come to two divergent
conclusions. And in regard to spiritual reality, the way to truth
is extremely complex, involving a whole spectrum of elements, not the least of which, as we have just mentioned
above, is the condition of purity and a proper spiritual attitude. Thus we would wish to point out in the beginning that
by pointing out the unity of method and the truly harmonious
results of biblical understanding and usage in the catholic
churches of East and West, we are not implying any sort of
automatic, guaranteed, easy-to-come-by conclusions in biblical
interpretation merely on the basis of an exegetical method
alone—especially one in which the name of the Holy Spirit is
involved. For biblical exegesis is not a matter of mechanical
implementation of a technical method. Nor is it a matter of
piety. Still less is it a matter of authority. It is a matter of
exercising the proper method in the proper way, with the
proper mental and spiritual activities necessary to produce
the proper result; which means, in a word, an objective interpretation of scripture within the totality, integrity and catholic
fulness of the Christian Church.

Generally speaking we would distinguish three main forms
of spiritual exegesis of the Bible from the perspective of the

[60]See Daniélou, *Origen,* p. 164.

wholeness of the Church. We find examples of such exegesis of the scripture in the Bible itself, especially in the New Testament writings, gospels and epistles alike, as well as in the earliest liturgies and apologetic writings. In the patristic age this type of exegesis flourished. The very flourishing produced, naturally, results of unequal value. However, all theology in this period, both the most fortunate and the least, operated within and on the basis of such a biblical exegetical approach. The liturgical services of the Church, both in form and content, also manifest the same approach to the Bible. These services still are used in the Orthodox Church today. Mention should be made also, as prime examples of this method of dealing with the scriptures, of catechetical-homiletical writings, often on liturgical-sacramental themes, as well as of ascetical-spiritual writings, which also exemplify forms of this general type of biblical interpretation.

The first type of spiritual-churchly exegesis we might call the way of immediate spiritual vision, intuition and understanding. It is the way of interpreting and understanding the Bible as a direct revelation of divine, spiritual reality; a way possible to man, as we have said above, due to man's spiritual nature as the image of God, capable of assimilating all attributes of the divine nature: life, knowledge, wisdom, truth, goodness . . . and especially (as is always listed as the highest perfection) love.

As a spiritual person, man can know spiritual reality. He can even "become" what he knows, becoming full of knowledge and truth and love to the extent that he is in communion with such realities, which is another way of saying to the extent that he retains and develops his nature as image and likeness of God. In reference to the Bible this means that when spiritual reality is revealed, man is capable of grasping this reality immediately and intuitively, to the measure, once more, of his total personal spiritualization and purification. Man can see and know and receive the knowledge of God directly. He can operate on this purely spiritual level without the need of formal concepts and logical abstractions removed from the reality itself. He can operate, so to speak, in the divine realm which is the ontological ground for every more

mediate, dialectical process of ratiocination. Thus, for example, when the Bible speaks of wisdom, truth, love, holiness and all those spiritual realities which are in their perfect
form attributes of God, and indeed when the Bible speaks of
God Himself, man has the ability as man to grasp these
realities directly, in experiential communion, in intuitive vision,
in his mind and in his heart. He can know directly what these
realities are, what they mean, how they exist, how they
interrelate. And still more. When the Bible discloses God
Himself, who is the one ultimately revealed in the biblical
events and words, in Christ and the Church in the Spirit, man
can truly know Him and be in union with Him to the extent,
once more, that God has revealed Himself and that man,
through purity of mind and heart, has received Him. To
deny that this is possible is to deny the Bible itself, which
claims that it is possible. It is to deny that Christ has come
from God and has given the Spirit to those who are being
saved.

This first form of churchly exegesis would probably be
very skeptical about what can be gained on this level from
historical, cultural, formal studies. It would just deny that
the spiritual realities spoken of and manifested in the Bible,
even in the Old Testament, are exhaustively known by such
studies. For example, it would surely reject the assertion that
when, for instance, the works attributed to the apostle John
mention love, the totality of insight possible is limited to the
idea of love of such a first- or second-century man, of such
cultural influences and such religious persuasions; and that
to gain the idea of love it is necessary to reconstruct and
relive the particular cultural, historical moment, and to analyse the formal structure of the scriptural text. Such studies
may be helpful, but they are neither exhaustive nor even, the
boldest position would hold, absolutely necessary. For man
can know love directly, particularly man in Christ and the
Spirit, in the Church, for whom the knowledge of love, the
same insight and experience and vision as that of the author
of the given text, is possible, accessible and indeed truly essential. In a word, man is called to know directly what the Bible
reveals and witnesses of spiritual, divine reality.

The other two forms of churchly exegesis in the Spirit are more complicated to discuss because of a confusion in terms and a confusion in actuality as well. One of these types of exegesis may be called *typological* and the other *spiritual-allegorical*.[61] Each of these types of exegesis deals primarily, but not exclusively, with biblical phenomena of external character: personalities, events, institutions. Each of them sees a progressive movement in the biblical story and record from the less perfect to the more perfect, from the partial to the fulfilled, from the material to the spiritual, from the *shadow* (to use the famous image of the Letter to the Hebrews) to the *reality*.[62] Each method of interpretation sees Christ as the scriptural, historical and spiritual center of the Bible. Each sees all things fulfilled in Him, in His Church and in His Kingdom. Each sees the Old Testament as the preparation for the New, with the New prefigured in the Old. Each sees the Church as the corporate experience of union with God in Christ and the Holy Spirit, which must be as well the personal experience of the individual soul. Each sees the primary purpose and insight of its particular interpretation as ultimately disclosing the ultimate reality of things: the reality of the Blessed Trinity itself.

We are not at all competent to develop the histories of these types of biblical interpretation. We only wish to try to show here, at least in a sketchy way, the meaning of these forms of biblical understanding in and for the Church, their reason for being, so to speak, and their relationship to each other and to the total life and experience of the Church.

Typological exegesis can be found in the Bible itself even in connection with the scriptural interpretation of Jesus.[63] According to this method of reading the scriptures, persons and events and institutions of scriptural history are seen to have a meaning which transcends their concrete meaning in their particular historical context, a meaning which relates

[61]DeLubac, Daniélou and Florovsky differ in their interpretations of these ways of interpreting the Bible. See particularly Daniélou, *Origen*, pp. 139-199; and Florovsky, "Revelation and Interpretation," pp. 168-180.

[62]Hebr. 10:1; Col. 2:17.

[63]*E.g.*, Matt. 12:38, 16:4; Lk. 11:29; Rom. 5:14; 1 Cor. 10:4; 1 Pet. 3:18; Hebrews.

to events of later times, particularly to the events of the New Testament, and so also the final realities of the Kingdom of God. Thus, at the depths of historical realities are found eternal realities, eternal realities which have a progressive unfolding and development in historical persons and happenings. Thus, for example, an event of the Old Testament "foreshadows" and "typifies" an event of the New Testament, which itself contains the revelation of an eternal truth, an aspect of the manifestation of God Himself. This way of reading the Bible presupposes that later generations have deeper insights into things than previous generations. It presupposes as well that there is an experience of reality available to later peoples which will allow them to see things in earlier occurrences which would be unknown and unknowable to those living at the time and even to those recording the scriptural testimony. This is more than simply presupposed: it is expressly taught in the Christian tradition that such a reading of the Bible is possible, and is exactly the necessary and correct one, because of the light and knowledge given in the Church of Christ and the Holy Spirit which "removes the veil" from the true meaning of the Old Testamental writings and allows them to be read with their real meaning, significance and prefigurative witness.[64]

There is no need to multiply examples of typological exegesis here since it is so common in the Church's tradition. Patristic writings of every sort are full of this type of biblical interpretation. The liturgy of the Church is formed and constituted by it. It is its most evident expression. The chief characteristic of this way of reading the Bible, as we have mentioned, is to see foreshadowings and prefigurations of the final events of the New Testament and of the Church in the life and record of the Old. Thus, for example, Old Testamental personalities like Adam, Melchizedek, Moses, Joshua, Job and Jonas are seen as related to Christ, "typical" of some aspect of His person and work and fully understandable in their fullest revelatory meaning only in relation to Him. Old Testamental theophanies are seen to prefigure the most

[64]2 Cor. 3:15-4:6. See also Basil the Great, *On the Holy Spirit* (Nicene and Post-Nicene Fathers, Second Series, vol. 8, p. 33).

perfect theophany, the incarnation of the Word of God in human flesh; thus, for example, the mariological interpretations of these texts in liturgical hymnology.[65] The passover-exodus foreshadowed in a material, historical way the death and resurrection of Christ, and the details of the typification are striking: liberation from slavery, suffering and death; the lamb, the blood, the sacrifice, the meal; passage through the sea, food from heaven, bread, water; the law, cloud, fire, light; the promised land. Sinai points to Pentecost, with cloud and fire and law, as does Babel in another prefigurative way. The priesthood, the sacrifices, the temple—these types are exposed in the Letter to the Hebrews. The wars of Israel foreshadow the spiritual struggle of the righteous, first of all Jesus Christ, against the principalities and powers of darkness. Again this is clearly shown by how the psalms are used in the New Testament Church.[66] Kingship and prophecy prefigure the King and the Prophet and the age in which all men are prophets and kings. Israel is the Church; Jerusalem, the Heavenly City.

As the Old Testament typifies the New, the New Testament Church typifies the Kingdom of God. In the Church, therefore, both the preparatory history and the most finalized eternal eschatology are brought together into unity; the former by way of fulfillment, the latter by way of anticipation in mystical, sacramental, symbolical presence. Since the liturgy is the most concrete expression of the Church's vision and life, being itself, one might say, the official life of the Church, one may expect to find here the Church's most official expression of its biblical character and understanding, the most official expression of its biblical interpretation. And indeed this is the case, and liturgical interpretation of the Bible is virtually totally typological.

The Bible is practically the sole source of the Church's

[65]For Old Testamental theophanies as types of the incarnation in mariological context see, *e.g.*, the matinal canons of the feasts of the Nativity, Dormition, and Introduction to the Temple of the Mother of God: *The Festal Menaion*, trans. Mother Mary and Kallistos Ware (London, 1969).

[66]See Athanasius, *On the Psalms, trans. cit.,* pp. 97-120. Also the introduction of Lazarus Moore to his translation of the Septuagint Psalter, *The Holy Psalter* (Madras, India, 1966).

liturgy, both in form and content. The liturgical pattern of
the Church, its cycles of feasting and fasting, of psalmody
and prayer; its sacramental rituals; its words, symbols and
images; its appreciation and utilization of matter and space
and time—all of this is expressly biblical. In both spirit and
flesh the liturgy is biblical. It is not as if the Bible were added
to the services and rites for purposes quite external, for further
explanation, information and edification. In the liturgy the
Bible comes alive to be what it must be and shows itself for
what it really is: the living Word of God for God's living
People.[67] It is in the liturgy that the People meet the Word.
And it is in the liturgy that the Word comes to His People.
It is in the liturgy that the Bible offers itself for exegesis;
and it is in the liturgy, as the most immediate realization of
the Church itself, that exegesis is accomplished. As we have
indicated, typological appreciation is central in liturgical use
of the Bible and in the very biblical character of the liturgy
itself, both in form and content, in the liturgy's shape as well
as in the direct use it makes of biblical texts in psalms, verses,
lections, quotations and adaptations in canons and hymns. For
the liturgy is the Church's common experience of that reality
prefigured in the Old Testament, fully realized in Christ and
the Spirit, given to human experience through communion
in the Church, finally realized cosmically at the end of the
ages in the Kingdom of God. We conclude, therefore, that
since the Church's liturgical appropriation and manifestation
of the Bible is essentially typological in both its form and
content, and since the liturgy is the most objective and official
expression of the vision and life of the Church as knowledge
and communion with God through Christ in the Holy Spirit,
then typological exegesis of the Bible, not merely as holy
history but as the progressive revelation of the most perfect
and eternal spiritual reality, is in fact the official exegetical
method of interpreting the Bible in the Church, particularly
the scriptures of the Old Testament; and that it is precisely
as prefigurations of the eternal truth given in Christ that the

[67]Daniélou, *The Bible and the Liturgy*. Also Schmemann, *Sacraments and Orthodoxy*, p. 37-39; J. Leclercq, *La Liturgie et le Paradoxe Chrétien* (Paris, 1963), esp. p. 284.

writings of the Old Covenant have their meaning and value.

Considering now the form of churchly, spiritual exegesis which we have called spiritual-allegorical, we must repeat a well-known fact: that this way of interpreting the Bible in the Church is the most individualistic and subjective one. If the typological method is abused by a too eager and enthusiastic desire to see "types" in the most unexpected places, and if there has been typological exegesis which has simply not found a place in the catholic tradition of the Church because of its forced and artificial character, then some of the examples of the moralizing, spiritualizing and allegorizing of biblical texts will be speedily rejected as indeed the result of unenlightened imagination and pure fantasy. We must note right away, however, that the rejection of certain allegorizing interpretations, as well as of certain typological ones, has been done by church tradition quite universally not in the name of another exegetical method, but because this use of the method has been unfaithful to the total experience of the Bible and the Church, incapable of being integrated in the proper way into its total vision and life. For at the same time that one can show that certain typological and allegorical interpretations are unacceptable to the catholic mind and spirit of the Church, one can also demonstrate that certain results of these same methods of biblical interpretation have been traditionally and universally accepted by the Church in various times and places. For there is a catholic tradition, not merely of typological exegesis, but of allegorical, spiritual exegesis as well.

Spiritual-allegorical exegesis is found almost exclusively in contexts dealing with the life of the individual soul, especially in treatises of ascetical or mystical theology, spirituality or morality. It is used in sermons as the means of revealing some aspect of the soul's relation with God, or the community's, in an especially spiritual or moral way. Since the soul is the most subjective aspect of the life of the Church, and indeed ultimately the most important, there should be no surprise that so much attention is given to it in Christian literature, and also that so much of the Bible is used in relation to it. There should be little surprise also that there is a preponderant amount of spiritualizing and moralizing and

allegorizing of biblical texts in the Church's tradition, and
that these uses of the Bible should be so individualistic and
subjectivistic, hardly universally applicable all the time to
everyone, everywhere.

The soul is the individual, subjective image of God; and
it is in an existential way also the image of Christ and the
image of the Church. What Christ has experienced with God
and man and the devil, the Church must experience, and each
individual must experience. If the Bible is centered in Christ
and fulfilled in Him and the Church, then it is also centered
in the human person, particularly the Christian, and fulfilled
in him as well. If the law and the prophets spoke of Christ,
then they speak of the soul as well. If Israel is the image of
Christ and the Church, then Israel—its history, struggles, sins,
repentances, sacrifices, prophecies, and everything in it and
about it—is the image of the soul as well. In this sense then—
and it seems to be the sense of the Church—the whole Bible
allegorizes the life of Everyman and relates to it directly on
the personal, spiritual, moral level. Creation, sin, repentance,
the external, legalistic, incomplete and not fully enlightened
ethic and worship by law, the final maturation in spiritual
adulthood, eternal life—this is the life of Everyman from birth
to eternity, for each one in some sense must pass through his
desert, his period of pedagogical development in obedience to
law, his entrance into the freedom of manhood. And so the
whole Bible, and of course certain specific parts of it more
than others, lends itself readily to spiritualistic and moralistic interpretation.

It would be incorrect to claim, however, that because of
the expressly subjective circumstances of this form of exegesis,
it is therefore simply arbitrary, whimsical and capricious,
simply the product of imaginings and fantasy, not "exegesis"
at all but merely the use of the Bible as a pretext for giving
one's own private opinion on something, however pious. It
would be wrong to make such general accusations against
this form of biblical interpretation (although once more it
must be admitted that abuses obviously exist) because there
are examples of such interpretation which are in the Church
and of the Church, formed and inspired by the total life of

the Church as it applies to the individual person. We must remember here again that the Spirit who inspires the Church and the Bible is the Spirit whose dwelling place is man, the individual man. That which the Spirit reveals of God through Christ in the Bible and the Church must finally come alive in the individual person. As long as the Bible is used directly for this purpose—as a collection of texts read and meditated upon in relation to the person, not in "private" but as a member of the Church—it will be understood and interpreted by the allegorical-spiritual method. There is no way of avoiding it; and there is no reason to do so.

Authentic churchly allegorical interpretation of the scriptures in a spiritualistic or moralistic way is a true expounding of the biblical text itself, a genuine interpretation of it, however subjective it might be. It is the attempt to discover what God is saying to the soul in Christ in the given passage. In the best traditional examples of this type of exegesis, this is expressly the case. The exegete is interested in the text. He examines the words and makes linguistic studies. He considers the variations of versions, the textual and contextual setting of the passage. He compares the passage and the various words in it to other passages, pointing out similarity and contrast. He is passionately concerned with knowing what God is saying to his soul in and through the biblical word. One may gravely doubt the success or the value of such uses of the Bible or such interpretations of it. But one may not doubt that those who have used such methods—and virtually every church father and every liturgy in East and West has done so—have done so legitimately, within a churchly context, with the intention of revealing the spiritualistic meaning of the text which the text itself actually contains and reveals. There is no doubt that those most interested in the soul, the spirit, and the interior and invisible world generally, have been most interested in using the Bible this way and that their very spiritualism, especially when inspired by a philosophy and vision of reality not in accord with that of the Bible and the Church, has led to deformations, to false interpretations, and in extreme cases to false doctrines, as in the case of the Origenists. However the facts of deviation and unbalance, which have always been checked and rejected by the Church, must not be permitted to compromise the valid churchly, catholic and orthodox use of the Bible in this spiritual, allegorical, moralistic way.[68]

It must be noticed also that hardly any allegorizing exegesis can be found in the Church in which its exponent does not disclaim any pretensions of giving the one and only universal exegesis of the biblical text in question. Almost always the author of such biblical interpretations says specifically that he is giving a personal interpretation, sometimes he gives more than one, and more often than not he invites the reader to offer his own.[69] Honesty demands that this point be taken into full consideration in relation to this type of biblical interpretation. At the same time, honesty requires the recognition that in the Church's tradition there does in fact exist a catholic tradition of allegorical exegesis, a tradition which has in almost every time and place interpreted the same texts in the same or very similar spiritualistic ways. The Canticle of Canticles commentaries are a prime example for demonstrating that this form of exegesis is not mere fancy or the result of the unbridled flow of the imagination in a whimsical way. For even if historical influences could be proved linking every similar example of allegorical exegesis (and we doubt that this can be done) this would not mean that the similarity in question was the result of blind, unenlightened custom, of traditionalism in the crudest and most slavish form. Such a conclusion, totally unexceptable on historical grounds alone, would also ignore the unity, freedom and truth of the Church which lives in every generation, particularly in its prophets and saints.[70]

The tradition of this type of exegesis also reveals that scriptural texts, particularly those most conducive to allegorical interpretation, have within themselves in their churchly

[68]See n. 49 *supra*.

[69]*E.g.*, Gregory of Nyssa, *Commentary on the Canticle of Canticles*, trans. Daniélou, *From Glory to Glory*, pp. 269-270.

[70]Gregory of Nyssa himself strictly condemns the tyranny of "irrational custom," *ibid.*, p. 161. And one can hardly imagine a Bernard of Clairvaux, for example, blindly following historical precedent in anything, including biblical interpretation.

setting a sort of built-in capacity for producing the same insights and the same reactions when interpreted in this sort of spiritualistic way. The examples here are many: erotic love in the Canticle of Canticles, the condition of captivity and liberation, exile and return, sacrifice, physical ascent, warfare, *etc.* Just considering the absolutely universal spiritualistic interpretations of the physical ascensions in the biblical record (Sinai, Horeb, Carmel, Tabor, Hermon, Golgotha, Olives) makes us conclude that it is not pure accident on the one hand, or historical determinism and blind traditionalism on the other, which has produced such unanimity of interpretation. It is more reasonable to conclude that God Himself, knowing the nature of the world and the soul, the physical and spiritual realities which He has created, is precisely interested in revealing a spiritual truth by means of the physical descriptions of ascent in the biblical writings, knowing that such readings would be done—and even inspiring them to be done, under the guidance of the Spirit in the Church. We submit that this is exactly the case, and that this is exactly the understanding of the catholic Church and the foundation of its catholic spiritualistic-allegoristic exegesis of the Bible.

In conclusion we would wish to point out once more that each of the forms of churchly spiritual exegesis (the directly intuitive way of understanding; the typological way in its more objective, communal, historical and liturgical context; and the allegorical-spiritual way, particularly in its relation to spirituality and mystical theology) are deeply and necessarily unified in the living life of the Church. None of them can be isolated and separated from the others, none can claim autonomy or superiority or exclusive standing in the Church. Together they form one way of biblical interpretation, the way inspired and demanded by the total life and vision and experience of the Christian Church.

In the Orthodox tradition it has been repeated many times that the Church is a way of life—life in the Holy Spirit. It has been formulated and proclaimed that the sole authority in the Church is God, the Spirit and the Lord. The temptations to locate another authority other than the Spirit in the wholeness of the Church has been formally rejected. Every "external criterion of truth" has been denied over and again, be it the Bible, council, magisterium, hierarchy, or one or another bishop or see. There is no secure, automatic way to the knowledge of God or to certain, infallible truth; there is no way but the way of Christ in the Spirit in freedom and love and purity, the way shown in the Bible and the Church's tradition, the way to be realized and fulfilled in freedom by every generation working out its salvation in fear and trembling with God at work within it.[71]

In relation to biblical exegesis and the use of the Bible in the Church, the position is just this one. The search for external criteria of biblical interpretation is a vain one. The attempt to construct formal principles of exegesis by which the certain understanding of the scriptures is automatically guaranteed, without reference to the total life, wisdom and experience of the Church, is a hopeless one. The Bible is understandable and interpretable solely within the integrity of the Church, in which all aspects of reality are brought together into organic and vital synthetic unity: God and man, this world and the world to come, this time and eternity. For the reality which the Bible reveals is the same reality which is alive in the Church: the reality of God making Himself known through the Word in the Spirit, the reality of creation knowing God through the same Word in the same Spirit. And the Bible, the Word of God inspired by the Spirit in its creation and interpretation, is the scriptural element within this catholic life of divine-human communion.

[71]See n. 2 *supra.*

3

Catholicity and Ecumenism

> *... the Church, which is His body, the
> fulness of Him who fills all in all.*
> —Eph. 1:23

1.

The Church, for Orthodox Christians, is first of all an object of faith. We believe in the Church as we believe in God the Father, the Lord Jesus Christ, and the Holy Spirit. As an object of faith the Church is a divine reality. We can only believe in what is divine. We cannot place our trust in anything creaturely. As a divine reality the Church is of God. It is not primarily, and certainly not merely, a human organization, something created and constituted solely by men, even if by the will of God. It is rather the gift of God to men of His own truth and love, of His very own life, the eternal life of the Most Blessed Trinity.

The Church is God's gift to men of communion and life with Himself: with the Father through the Son in the Holy Spirit. The Church is the gift of life *within* the Blessed Trinity by means of divine power and grace, the uncreated divine energies which flow essentially and eternally from the three divine persons and are communicated to men always and forever from the person of the Father, through the person of the Son and Word, in the person of the Holy Spirit. Just as the uncreated Trinity is one and holy, so the Church of the

Trinity is one and holy. And as the uncreated Trinity is
catholic, i.e., full, complete, whole, perfect, all-embracing,
lacking nothing of the superabundance of all that is good,
holy, beautiful and true—so the Church of the Trinity is
catholic, essentially and by definition: full, complete, whole,
perfect, all-embracing, lacking nothing of the inexhaustible
fulness and superabundance of the very nature and life of
God.[1]

As the unity and holiness of the Church depend solely on
God and can neither be created nor destroyed by any creaturely power, so the catholicity of the Church is exactly the
same. The essential catholicity of the Church of Christ can
neither be created nor destroyed, increased nor diminished
by the will or action of anything creaturely—neither by angels
(demons) nor men. The Church is catholic by nature because
it is of God and from God, the gracious gift of God to men
in all times and places of full communion with Himself, and
with all things in heaven and on earth in Him.

As God's gift to men of His very own life in His Son
Jesus Christ by the grace of the Holy Spirit, the Church has
a very definite content and form. The Church is not invisible
nor unlocatable in space and time. We can know where the
Church is. We can discover it, enter into it, become part of
it and be certain that *here* is the Kingdom of God. We can
discover the Church in all its fulness in this world because
the Church, with Christ its Head, has been incarnated in the

---

[1]See N. Afanasieff, "The Church Which Presides in Love," *The Primacy
of Peter in the Orthodox Church* (London, 1963), pp. 57-110; G. Florovsky,
"Sobornost: The Catholicity of the Church," *The Church of God,* ed. Mascall
(London, 1934), pp. 54-74, "The Church: Her Nature and Task," *The Uni-
versal Church in God's Design* (Amsterdam I; London, 1948), pp. 42-58,
"The Doctrine of the Church," *The Ecumenical Review* 2 (1950), pp. 152-
161; A. Khomiakov, *The Church Is One* (New York, 1953); V. Lossky, *The
Mystical Theology of the Eastern Church* (London, 1957), "Catholic Con-
sciousness: The Anthropological Implication of the Dogma of the Church,"
St. Vladimir's Theological Quarterly 14 (1970), pp. 187-195; J. Meyendorff,
Orthodoxy and Catholicity (New York, 1966), "The Orthodox Concept of the
Church," *St. Vladimir's Theological Quarterly* 6 (1962), pp. 59-71. See also
the excellent ecumenical statement of the Joint Working Group of the Roman
Catholic Church and the World Council of Churches on the theme "Catholicity
and Apostolicity" prepared in Rome in 1968 (Faith and Order Paper No. 59,
Geneva, 1971), pp. 136-138.

life of our world and possesses a genuinely human content and form.

A Theandric Mystery

The Church exists in space and time and is manifested in the world as the incarnation and epiphany of God in His people, through Christ and the Holy Spirit. The Church is given to men and is realized in and through them as the mystery of the Kingdom of Heaven in the midst of the earth, or, as St. Gregory of Nyssa put it, as the mystical "recreation of the world."[2] The Church's incarnate expression in the world is sacramental and mystical, and so it is truly eschatological and belongs to God's kingdom.[3] The Church is fundamentally and essentially a *theandric mystery*. It is the mystery of the Most Holy Trinity and God's Kingdom, the mystery of God assuming, possessing, and interacting in gracious freedom with human persons and institutions. It is not fundamentally a human organization or institution, a society of men assuming, possessing and utilizing the sacred mysteries of God.

One discovers the Church in the space and time of this world as a sacramental reality, a divine reality with a human form made divine by grace. The humanity of the Church is deified by the Spirit of Christ. It is a humanity made "adequate to God" through the flesh of Christ which is itself made divine not merely by grace, but by the incarnation of the Word who assumed it and made it His own. Although the humanity of the Church strictly requires the free and gracious collaboration of men whose persons are not divine, unlike that of the Word Incarnate, there is still an analogy between Christ's incarnation in His own person, and His embodiment and incorporation in the multitude of created persons in the Church. The analogy, as we are concerned with it here, consists in the fact that in the Church, as in the Lord, it is *God*

[2] St. Gregory of Nyssa, *Commentary on the Canticle of Canticles*, PG 44: 1049B.

[3] See G. Florovsky, "The Church: Her Nature and Task," p. 54; also V. Lossky, *Mystical Theology*, pp. 156-157, 164-168, *et passim*.

who takes the initiative to assume and to save humanity; it
is not *man* who is the prime acting subject, assuming and
dealing with things divine.[4]

The deified form of the Church is, as we have said, sacramental and eschatological. By this we mean that in the
Church, God is living and acting in men by grace, expressing
and manifesting Himself and His Kingdom in gracious collaboration with human persons, in human words, symbols,
structures and forms which are, within the bounds of their
human limitations, adequate and proper to His divinity. This
means that the Church *as Church* is located in this world as
a theandric reality, the mystery of the synergy of God and
man in the divinized world where God's grace and man's
response meet in perfect freedom and harmony, so that God's
own most fundamental and unwavering intention for the
world in His gracious acts of creation, redemption and glorification will be accomplished and He will Himself be—as He
has desired it from all eternity through Christ—"all and in
all" (Col. 3:11).

All of the human members, offices, institutions, ministries
and agencies of the Church exist and operate only for this
purpose, that the Kingdom of God might be present and
powerful in the world and that Christ might be "all and in
all." They all find their origin and purpose in terms of the
divine mystery of the Kingdom which they exist to reveal and
to make manifest and mighty in the midst of the earth, which
mystery continually guides and judges them in all that they
do. Thus it is the divine mystery of the Holy Trinity living
and acting in the world through the Church which determines
and judges the thoughts, words and deeds of the Church's
human members and institutions; it is not the human members and institutions of the Church which determine and
judge its divine character and form. In a word, it is the
Church headed by Christ and led by the Spirit which governs,
guides and saves man and his world; it is not man and his
world which govern, guide and save the Church.

One discovers the Church on earth to be a sacramental

---

[4]G. Florovsky, "Christ and His Church: Suggestions and Comments,"
L'Église et les églises (Chevtogne, 1954), p. 167.

reality, and one enters the Church by sacramental mystery. Discovery of the Church, as well as entrance into it and abiding within it as the mystical community of the Kingdom of God on earth, depends on *faith* in the revelation of God in Christ and the Spirit known through the Church, and on the continual *conversion of life* in obedience to God, which is in its integrity a life lived in conformity to Christ by the power of the Holy Spirit. Thus the Church's presence in the world as a sacramental mystery cannot possibly be understood mechanistically or ritualistically as if the Church were merely a cultic community devoid of a very specific doctrine and ethical life.

The contents of the Christian Church are the truth and love of God. Without divine truth and love there is no Church. It is in order to give men His truth and love that God the Father sends His Son and His Spirit to the world. The truth and love of God are the gifts of God and depend solely on Him. God's truth and love are the very being and life of the Church, the very substance and content of its catholic fulness and integrity as the "union of faith and of love."[5] When one enters the Church he enters into communion with the fulness of divine truth and love. When one separates himself from the Church he separates himself from the fulness of divine truth and love. Neither the addition of members to the Church nor the separation of persons from the Church affects the mystical essence of the Church as God's gift of Himself to men.

There is nothing that can be added to the essential being of the Church by men, and nothing that can be taken from it. The catholic fulness of the Church depends on God alone. Men may be faithful or unfaithful, but God remains faithful, and His truth and love abide steadfast forever. Men may be united to the Church or divided from it, but they may neither unite nor divide the Church, which remains one and undivided by the grace of the Trinity. Men may participate in the Church with faith and love for the forgiveness of sins and life everlasting, or they may participate in the Church as unfaithful and unloving for their condemnation and judgment, or they

[5]St. Ignatius of Antioch, *Magnesians* 1:2.

may not participate at all—but the Church remains forever essentially the same: the mystery of the Kingdom of God revealed and given to men in Christ and the Spirit, the divine gift of salvation and life everlasting for those who believe.

As the fulness of divine life communicated to men, the Church can never be totally identified with its earthly members and institutions. The Church of God is not coextensive with its creaturely members nor is it exhausted in its being and membership by them. Besides angels and saints, including the Theotokos as the most perfectly deified member and as such the very "icon of the Church,"[6] the Body includes in its membership Christ Himself as its Head, and the Holy Spirit as its vivifying, sanctifying and deifying power. The Church is the Body of Christ animated by the Holy Spirit. It is the "fulness of deity bodily" (Col. 2:9), by grace and not by nature. It is the fulness of divine life given to men as a gift toward which each individual member must grow personally and in communion with all other persons and the whole of creation. It is the fulness and perfection which can never be fully and perfectly achieved by men, neither in this age nor in the Kingdom to come, since it is indeed the fulness and perfection of God Himself—"the Church, which is His body, the fulness of Him who fills all in all" (Eph. 1:23).[7]

Stability and Dynamism

Men in God, and so in the Church, are always *in via,* for Christ who is the truth and the life is also the *way,* and the way is endless since it is the way of knowledge and communion and life with the infinite, incomprehensible, uncontainable and—perfectly—unattainable God. Within the stability of the Kingdom of God, which is fully revealed and given to men in the Church, there is thus an existential dynamism. It is the dynamism of eternal life which is only accessible to

[6]See V. Lossky, *Mystical Theology,* pp. 193-195; Ouspensky and Lossky, *The Meaning of Icons* (Boston, 1953), p. 78.

[7]See G. Florovsky, "The Church: Her Nature and Task," p. 54; Lossky, *Mystical Theology,* pp. 174-195; also Florovsky's critique of Lossky's positions in "Christ and His Church: Suggestions and Comments," p. 168.

men within the stability of the gracious salvation of Christ's Body, the stability which is made firm on the Rock of Christ and yet is eternally dynamic by the breathing of the Holy Spirit.[8]

Within the Church, therefore, there are two necessary and deeply interconnected and undivided aspects. There is the aspect of the Church's *givenness* by God, its firm and stable mystical *being* in Christ and the Spirit. And there is at the same time that aspect of the Church's *reception* by men, its dynamic and ever-moving existential *becoming* in Christians by the same Christ and the same Spirit. Thus in the Church, at one and the same time, there is the fulness and perfection of divine truth and love, the very life of God present in Christ and the Spirit, and there is the appropriation and attainment of the divine truth and love of God ever more perfectly by the creaturely members of the Church who, by Christ and the Spirit, are in the unending process of becoming "gods by grace."[9] Thus once more, the catholicity of the Church is an essential characteristic of the Church given to it by God to be acquired by men always and necessarily in a partial and incomplete way because of the created nature of men, who are indeed not capable of attaining perfectly to the absolute superabundant nature of God. The partiality and incompleteness of the human members of the Church, not to speak of their outright sins which in fact separate them from the Church, does not affect the essential catholic being of the Church, which is guaranteed to it not by the works of men but by the grace of God. Thus, although it is perfectly accurate and correct to contend that the Church may be built up by men, that it may grow and prosper, or on the contrary, that it may diminish and weaken, it must be clearly understood that these expressions have to do not with the divine aspect of the Church as given and guaranteed to it by God, but with the existential appropriation of divinity in the actual

[8] See St. Gregory of Nyssa, *The Life of Moses*, PG 44:405A-D. Also on this point see J. Daniélou and H. Musurillo, *From Glory to Glory* (New York, 1961), pp. 56-71; L. Thunberg, *Microcosm and Mediator* (Lund, 1965), p. 448 ff.

[9] Lossky, *Mystical Theology*, p. 117; Daniélou, *loc. cit.*

lives and experiences of the Church's human members.[10] Thus
the members of the Church may more or less successfully
realize and manifest the unity, holiness, catholicity and apostolicity of the Church as a matter of existential fact, but this
realization and manifestation cannot be taken as determining
in any way what the Church is in its mystical divine reality
as the object of Christian faith, as God's gift to the world
which has, in its scriptures, doctrines, sacraments, saints and
canonical structures, a "human form" which is truly adequate
and proper to God.

2.

The Orthodox Church understands itself to be the one,
holy, catholic and apostolic Church, the true Church of Christ
on earth. This does not mean, as I have already indicated
relative to catholicity, that the fulness of divine life exists
perfectly and completely in any creaturely member or institution of the Church, nor in all creaturely members and institutions of the Church added together both in heaven and on
earth. Neither does this mean that the Church as a phenomenon in space and time is essentially identical with the catholic
fulness of the body of the incarnate Word in which has
dwelt and continues to dwell "all the fulness of deity bodily"
(Col. 2:9). It does mean, however, that because of Christ
and the Holy Spirit personally living and acting in the Church
and thus making it to be indeed the mystical body of Christ
by grace, there is a humanity "proper to God" revealed in
the mystical being of the Church, and thus in the Church the
way is fully open, already now in this age, for human persons
to grow in the perfection and fulness of the truth and love of
God, and so to become indeed "partakers of the divine
nature" (2 Pet. 1:4).

In the Orthodox Church—and this is the sole basis for the
confession of its belief to be the one, holy, catholic and

---

[10]St. Paul and the fathers of the Church are unanimous in making this
clear distinction. See Ephesians; 1 Corinthians 1, 11-14; St. John Chrysostom,
Homilies on First Corinthians 3, 24-35; St. Gregory of Nyssa, *Commentary
on the Canticle of Canticles*, PG 44:1045D-1052A.

apostolic Church of God—man's way to perfect and ever more perfect communion with God for eternity is already completely and fully open. In the Orthodox Church right now on earth, men can begin to live the unending life of God's heavenly Kingdom, in the knowledge of the true God and of Jesus Christ whom He has sent, and in the love of the Father and the Son made accessible to men in the Holy Spirit. Within the community of the Church men can be firmly rooted and grounded already now in the unending process of eternal deification.

In confessing itself to be the one catholic Church of God, the Orthodox Church identifies itself with the one catholic Church in history and claims that there is an absolute identity and continuity of this Church from the time of the apostles to the present day. The Orthodox Church identifies the catholic Church in history as the apostolic Church which is witnessed to in the canonical New Testament scriptures, the Church of the seven ecumenical councils, and the Orthodox Church of the East which continues to exist today in separation from the Western churches of Rome and the Reformation. Only in this Church do the Orthodox recognize the absolute identity and completely unbroken continuity of the catholic faith and life of the one Church of Christ.

The Orthodox Church affirms the legitimacy and necessity of its separation from all other Christian confessions on the basis of its inability to identify itself, and so the catholic Church of all ages, with these communions. The Orthodox Church cannot recognize itself in other Christian groups because, in its opinion, they contain formal and official confessional obstacles, distortions and deviations in essential doctrines and practices which block man's way to perfect communion with God when they are accepted and practiced. In these communions the catholic fulness of Christ, the fulness of grace and truth, has been lost. A member of any one of these communions will necessarily be frustrated and led astray from perfect communion with God and man to the extent that he makes his own and builds his life upon those elements in his particular confessional community which are incorrect or insufficient. In a word, the Orthodox claim that there exist in these bodies "human forms" which are not adequate or proper to God.

The loss of perfect fulness in the Church, its divine catholicity, is exactly what the Orthodox Church does not admit about itself in its claim to be the one, holy, catholic and apostolic Church of Christ. The Orthodox Church denies to itself any formal and official deviations, diminuations or distortions of any aspects of the "fulness of life" to which men have come in Christ (Col. 2:10; Jn. 1:3, 16; Eph. 1:23). It claims on the contrary, despite all of the weaknesses, deficiencies and sins of its members, that the Orthodox Church alone, in all that it formally and officially teaches and practices, remains perfectly faithful to the catholic fulness of God given to His Church, the fulness of the Most Holy Trinity.

The catholicity of the Orthodox Church, which forces it into separation from other Christian communions because of the absence of an essential identity of Christian faith and life with them, is the same factor which compels the Orthodox to affirm in other Christian bodies—and indeed when possible, in all religions and philosophies and in all human thoughts and actions—what is positively true and good in them. Because the Orthodox Church understands itself to be the catholic Church of Christ in which sinful and unworthy men become communicants and participants of "all the fulness of God" (Eph. 3:19, Col. 1:19), it is compelled by its very nature and vocation not only to "hate what is evil" and to separate itself from it, but "to prove what the will of God is, what is good and acceptable and perfect" (Rom. 12:2).

As catholic, therefore, the Orthodox Church cannot possibly deny all grace and truth to those outside of itself. It most particularly cannot dare to affirm that in other Christian communities, to whatever extent they are truly Christian, there is only darkness and error. The Orthodox Church must justly affirm that certain elements of the catholic fulness of God, revealed and given to the catholic Church through Christ and the Spirit, do remain in other Christian communities, that persons in these communities do hunger and thirst for this fulness, and that not seldom the most authentic elements of genuine Christianity are preached and practiced by non-Orthodox Christians with a fervor and power exceeding that of the members of the Orthodox Church themselves.[11] Since it is obvious as well that all Christian communities find their origin in the one catholic Church of Christ, it is the duty of the members of the Church which is truly catholic to restore all Christian persons and groups to their proper and necessary God-given fulness. In a word, therefore, it is the same catholicity of the Orthodox Church which requires it to preserve itself in official sacramental separation from the non-Orthodox communions, in which the fulness of Christian faith and life does not exist and whose human institutions and forms are not proper to God, which at the same time compels the Orthodox Church to recognize these bodies as originally of the catholic Church, possessing, practicing and preaching many things in common with it and so to enter into ecumenical relations with them in the difficult and painful, yet God-inspired and God-willed effort to restore them to the catholic fulness of the Church of the Most Blessed Trinity.

The restoration of the catholic fulness, without deviation, diminution or distortion, to all Christian communities is that which alone can make them one in Christ and one with the catholic Church of Christ. The express purpose of the ecumenical movement for the Orthodox Church is to restore the unity of all Christian bodies on the basis of the perfect identity of all of them with the catholic Church of Christ, "which is His body, the fulness of Him who fills all in all" (Eph. 1:23). Thus it is the goal of the Orthodox in the ecumenical movement, and the sole reason for their participation, to restore all Christian persons and groups to full and perfect unity with the Orthodox Church, and so with each other, with the catholic Church of history, with the victorious Church of the Kingdom of God, and we must add, with God

---

[11]Otherwise how could one possibly explain the fact that many persons have been received into the Orthodox Church from non-Orthodox Christian churches without baptism in the Orthodox Church, and also the fact that the Orthodox Church has canonized Constantine the Great and Isaac of Syria? See also Florovsky, "The Orthodox Church and the Ecumenical Problem," p. 156.

Himself: Father, Son and Holy Spirit. Only catholic unity in
the Trinity, unity in the catholicity of God, can make the
many churches one. Any other unity will not be and cannot
be the true Christian unity of the one holy Church, the unity
for which Christ not only prayed, but for which He assumed
human flesh and was crucified in order to be raised in the
glory of the Father.

Until the final and full restoration of catholic unity takes
place—and it may well take place only in the Kingdom to come
when the "fulness of God" which now mystically fills the
Church will fill all creation and Christ will be "all and in all"
(Col. 3:11)—it remains the ecumenical mission of Orthodoxy
to defend the reality of God's gift of catholicity to His Church,
and so to defend "whatever is true, whatever is honorable,
whatever is just, whatever is pure, whatever is lovely, whatever is gracious, if there is any excellence . . . anything worthy
of praise" (Phil. 4:8) wherever, whenever and in whomever
these realities actually exist. And still more, it remains the
task of the Orthodox to be in good-willed relations with all
Christians and all men to the extent that these realities exist
among them. For where these realities are already shared by
men, to that extent unity already exists among them; it need
only be recognized, expressed and celebrated. But where
these realities are not shared by men, we must add once more,
unity does not exist among them, no matter how fervently it
is desired, how sincerely it is sought, and how enthusiastically
it is proclaimed and celebrated. In this case the only realistic
and ultimately constructive thing to do is to acknowledge
the division and to work for its removal in the spirit of
humble honesty and repentance before God.

3.

The general vision of the catholicity of the Church presented here, together with its crucial implication for the life
of the Orthodox Church, both within itself and in its ecumenical activity, is not shared by all members of the Orthodox
Church today. There are those in the Orthodox Church who

do not see the Orthodox Church essentially as the divine presence of the Kingdom of God in human forms on earth, the mystery of the fulness of divine being and life, truth and love, dwelling in the community of human persons headed by Christ and animated by His Spirit, the community which is dogmatically and spiritually identical and continuous in history as the gracious incarnation in men of all the fulness of divinity, and whose essential content and form is sacramental and mystical. There are those rather who wittingly or unwittingly have accepted the view of the Church as essentially an organization of men which assumes and possesses the things of God, and not as the divine mystery of the Holy Trinity assuming and saving all things human.

The view of the Church as essentially an organization of men dealing with divine realities has many different existential forms. It ranges from the appreciation of the Church as a most highly structured authoritarian, juridicial society instituted and established by Christ and existing and operating by divine right as the exclusive dispenser of God's grace to the world, to the understanding of the Church as the collection of the most unstructured, free-acting and free-thinking groups of individuals united together by not much more than their common will to be together and to consider themselves as *church.* Both of the extreme positions just described, whatever the disagreements that exist between them, share what is fundamentally and essentially the same ecclesiological perspective, as do the many positions which exist between them. They all agree on one indisputable point: *the Church itself is not the mystery.* Whatever its form, structure, authority, content and mission, the Church is exhausted in its reality by its human aspect and form, which belong exclusively to this world and not to God's Kingdom, even though it is often understood to be—whether juridically or charismatically—established by God Himself and acting in His name and by His authority. Thus the Church in this view possesses doctrines, sacraments, worship, ethical practices. It contains these things. It proclaims and propagates them. It administers and directs them. It employs and uses them—again by whatever means and authority—but these things in themselves are *other* than what the Church *is*. They have no ontological ecclesial significance. They are extraneous to the Church's *being*.

Thus, as an example of this perspective, the sacramental life of the Church, with its doctrinal foundations and its spiritual implications, is considered to be something which the Church *has* or *does*. It is not considered as that which the Church *is*. The Church as organization, to continue the example, possesses and performs the mystery of the holy eucharist. It possesses and utilizes it, administers and practices it as a holy act, something "meet and right" for Christians to do. Within this common perspective there can be many disagreements and differences over how this holy act is to be done. Who does it? When? Where? Why? Under what conditions? By what authority? In what form? By what means? For what purposes? The questions are endless. But on one issue there can be no debate, namely that the mystery of the holy eucharist has no direct and immediate ontological relationship to the being and essence of the Church, that it is irrelevant to the Church's nature and insignificant to the Church's confessed reality of being one, holy, catholic and apostolic. Thus there can be, and there are, many discussions and debates within this perspective about the ecumenical issues of communion and intercommunion, open and closed communion, conditional and occasional communion, dynamic and static communion—all in terms of authorities, powers, forms and even "theologies" of the eucharistic action itself. But there can be no debate with the fundamental dogma agreed upon by all of this persuasion, namely that the mystery of the holy eucharist is not essentially related to the very being of the Church, that it is not essentially related to the fulness of the Church's doctrinal and spiritual life as well as to its sacramental-structural organizational form, and that therefore it is not expressive of the nature of the Church as the perfect gift of divine unity, holiness, fulness of truth and love, and concrete identity and continuity in space and time. Those who share this view of the Church will not understand those who defend the view of the Church and its catholicity presented here, in which, on the issue of communion and intercommunion, the only possible position must be that there can only be *communion,* and that this communion can only be in the one catholic Church, because this is what the Church *is.* The eucharist in the Church, together with all sacraments, doctrines, structures and spiritualities, must be expressive of the Church's catholic essence as the full and perfect unity and communion of men in "all the fulness of God" (Eph. 3:19). Thus, in this latter perspective, for the catholic Church such things as intercommunion, open, closed, partial, conditional, and occasional communion are ontologically—and not merely juridically or devotionally—impossible. Once again it is a question not of authority or of piety; it is a question of what the Church is, why it exists, and what it should be, realize and witness to in the world.[12]

The Denominationalist View

It is sadly true that the view of the Church as essentially an organization of men dealing with things divine, whether juridicially or charismatically, authoritatively or freely, has entered the Orthodox Church today and has created within the membership of the Church the whole spectrum of positions which this fundamental perspective allows within itself and to which it inevitably leads. Thus we have among the Orthodox today the two extremes of this same viewpoint, which for want for better terms and in the danger of creating unwanted confusion I will call the *denominationalist* position on the one side and the *sectarian* position on the other.

The *denominationalist,* whatever his confession or communion, recognizes not merely the existential value, but the essential necessity for many different church organizations to exist. He would affirm that each of these organizations must exist because each has some particular "contribution" to make, for each expresses in some partial way something of

[12]See my article, "The Eucharist and the Church," *The American Ecclesiastical Review* 164:6 (1971), pp. 373-383; G. Florovsky, "Terms of Communion in the Undivided Church," *Intercommunion,* ed. Baille and Marsh (New York and London, n.d.), pp. 47-57; J. Meyendorff, *Orthodoxy and Catholicity,* p. 155.

the catholicity of the universal Church, which has no struc-
tural expression of its own in the world and is therefore invisible and unlocatable in time and space. The denominationalist believes in the one, holy, catholic and apostolic Church,
but this Church exists nowhere in the world. What does exist
are denominations, each of which is judged to be limited and
partial not merely because of the actual existential limitations
of its members, both individually and corporately, but because
it is partial essentially—in its very nature, being and life. The
doctrine, sacraments, structures and spiritual practices of the
denomination—its "human form"—not only do not embody
and express the fulness of divine being and life which is
present in the Church and is then only partially and im-
perfectly appropriated by its members and member communities, but are in themselves partial and imperfect by nature and are not at all expected to be either expressions of or
ways to "all the fulness of God." Thus not only is any given
local church or denomination, not to mention the concrete
parochial assembly, existentially limited as a matter of fact
by the creatureliness and indeed sinfulness of its human members who obviously cannot possibly actualize the fulness of
divine life, but it is essentially limited in its very *being*,
in its *faith* and in its *order*, and as such is not expressive of
the catholicity of the Church, which is indeed believed in and
confessed by Christians but which is fully accessible to men
in no actually existing ecclesial community.

    In this general view, catholicity is always understood as
the sum total of the various forms and expressions of the
various Christian faiths and orders, with different advocates
of the general tendency drawing their lines at different points
as to where these forms cease to be authentic and valid. Some
would include, for various reasons, only certain of the Christian communions as expressive and constitutive of the "catholic Church," namely those of the "catholic tradition." Others
would include all Christian groups. And still others would
go further to understand genuine catholicity as exceeding
the boundaries of the Christian confessions and embracing
virtually all religions, philosophies and cultures. This latter
type would say that the Church, in its essential reality and

not merely in its existential realization and expression, grows in catholicity as it embraces a wider range of human social and cultural traditions.[13]

The denominationalists in the Orthodox Church today accept the general view just described and differ within it only according to its own allowable inner variations. All of them would agree not to permit the Orthodox Church to claim that it is the one, holy, catholic and apostolic Church of Christ, with the corresponding denial of this claim to others. They would agree on this point because for all of them the Orthodox Church is a human historical, existential phenomenon which is obviously partial, limited and incomplete. Identifying the Church of God totally and exclusively with its human form, with its external organizational boundaries, its customs and traditions, its cultural patterns and practices, the denominationalist would see the Orthodox Church as essentially an Eastern church, an oriental expression and form of the universal Christian Church of which it is but a part. The sacramental structure of the Church, including the hierarchy as well as the doctrines, canons and spiritual practices, would not be considered as *catholic* in the sense that, limited though they be, they still exist to make present and powerful in the world all the fulness of the Kingdom of God. They would be viewed rather as *denominational,* since they contain and reveal what is essentially incomplete and imperfect and thus can make no pretensions of being catholic in and of themselves.

In intra-Orthodox relations, following this same line of thought, those of denominationalist tendencies among the Orthodox would have no problem in viewing each local Orthodox church as a particular ethnic or cultural expression of the universal Christian Church, each with its own particular privileges, powers and prestige. They would even point to the various "national Orthodoxies" as examples of the "catholic" character of the Orthodox Church as a whole, once again however not at all because each of the various local Orthodox churches would each be expressive in its own unique way of

[13]See *Drafts for Sections, Uppsala, 1968* (Geneva, n.d.), pp. 1-27, *Uppsala Speaks* (Geneva, 1968), pp. 7-20.

something irreplaceable and otherwise undiscoverable of the "fulness of God" which is perfectly open to it and available in it because it *is,* in its sacramental mystical essence, the catholic Church of Christ. Instead each local church would be considered as "catholic" because the particular characteristics of its ecclesiastical life can be added to all others in which these particular traits are absent, and so it can comprise with them the universal Christian Church. Thus, very logically in such a perspective, within the Orthodox Church itself bishops can become ethnarchs and not "images of God,"[14] multiple ecclesiastical "jurisdictions" can overlap and even compete in the same geographical territory, church institutions, including not only the sacramental offices of the episcopate and priesthood but the whole of the theological, sacramental and spiritual life of the Church, can become tools for the propagation and preservation of cultures and traditions which are by definition partial, incomplete and essentially opposed to the catholic fulness of life and unity in the Kingdom of God given in Christ and the Holy Spirit. Thus, in this view, the Church in the world is not at all the sign and witness and bearer of God's eternal Kingdom in every aspect of its being and life, and any attempt to relate ecclesiastical structures, the "human form" of the Church (hierarchy, sacraments, dogmas, canons, *etc.*), to the Kingdom of God, *i.e.,* to view them as having a genuinely catholic significance, is absolutely rejected.

In addition to this, and once more following logically from it, the denominationalists in the Orthodox Church would categorically deny that Orthodoxy is for all men in all times and places, and would deny the Orthodox Church to certain peoples and cultures on the grounds that their particular human characteristics are incompatible with Orthodoxy in that they do not coincide with its "oriental ethos." It is such a position which not only disbelieves, for example, that Americans can become Orthodox—and remain Americans—but which also forms the basis for defending the denominationalist approach in ecumenical relations between the Orthodox and other Christians.

[14]St. Ignatius of Antioch, *Trallians* 3:1.

Generally speaking, those of denominationalist tendencies among the Orthodox would urge the Orthodox Church to unite with other Christians—with which ones and in what manner depending upon the particular denominationalist position which is held—not only so that a better, more complete, more perfect existential expression of the fulness of divine truth and life could exist in its human form more perfectly upon the earth, not only so that more persons could come to communion with the truth and love of God, not only so that the scandal of Christian division could be overcome—but precisely and expressly because the Orthodox Church in itself is essentially and by definition a partial and incomplete church, a *denomination,* with no just claim to be in its essential doctrinal, sacramental and spiritual integrity the one holy Church of Christ.

In ecumenical relations the denominationalists among the Orthodox might logically be quite willing for the Orthodox to be "in communion" with other Christian communities—again the exact manner of this communion being determined by the particular denominationalist position which is held—in the absence of complete identity of faith and life because such an identity cannot possibly exist between denominations which by nature are essentially different and necessarily dissimilar. Hence in the ecumenical movement allowance must be made not only for cultural and historical diversity and plurality of expressions and forms but for differences in faith and order as well. The fulness of doctrinal, sacramental and spiritual identity, and a Christian unity based on such an identity of fulness, is precisely what is denied to divided Christians in the denominationalist view. For the denominationalist the catholic Church does not exist as a concrete reality in this world. It is believed in as an ideal, but it does not exist historically.

The Sectarian View

Those of the opposite extreme from the denominationalists are those whom I have called the *sectarians* and who, I have insisted, hold fundamentally the same ecclesiological perspective as the denominationalists. The sectarians differ from their denominationalist brothers only as to where to draw the line where any and all expressions of catholicity end. The sectarians simply draw the line at the end of their own ecclesiastical organization.

Like the denominationalists, the sectarians view the Church primarily and essentially as a human organization. The human organization of the Church for the sectarians, however, exists by the express will of God in every detail of its content and form. It is divinely established and instituted in this world and possesses in and by itself all the fulness of the grace and truth of God existentially and exclusively.

The sect alone is the catholic Church. It alone is holy. This is *not,* however, understood to mean that within the true Church the fulness of divine truth and love, "all the fulness of God," is fully present and accessible to the human members without formal obstacles or errors of any kind which in fact do exist in other confessions, although the members of the catholic Church must recognize their own individual existential incompleteness, as well as what is truly of God and His Church outside of their own churchly organization, particularly in the Christians to whom catholic fulness is lacking. It is rather understood in the sense that the Church itself in the smallest details of its concrete existence in the world is such an organization that outside of itself there is and can be literally nothing of God and nothing of God's catholic Church. Outside of the jurisdiction of the true Church, for those of the sectarian attitude, there can only be utter darkness and error: the apostasy of Antichrist.

In a word, genuine catholicity remains for the sectarian as for the denominationalist the sum total of the valid institutional forms and expressions of the true Christian faith. It remains identified totally and exclusively with the human form of the Church, but where the denominationalist includes a number of institutional organizational forms—how many and which depending upon his particular convictions—the sectarian necessarily includes only one—his own.

Those of sectarian tendencies in the Orthodox Church

today apply this position rigorously. Not only do they logically deny that ecumenical activity is possible for the Orthodox since such activity presupposes that there is at least some common Christian ground between the Orthodox and non-Orthodox, but even within the Orthodox Church they assert their juridical, organizational position with steadfast consistency, calling all not only to "true Orthodoxy" or to the "true Church" but even to the "true jurisdiction."

The sectarians feel free, again quite logically according to their perspective, to identify the true faith and the true Church with the true jurisdictional organization—which of course is their own. Thus for them, exactly as for the denominationalists, the Church is not essentially the fulness of the Kingdom of God on earth which exists with all power and perfection in those human forms which are "proper to God" and preserved by Him in spite of the personal sins and errors of the Church's human members—sins and errors which do not affect the nature of the Church as one, holy, catholic and apostolic. For the sectarians as for the denominationalists the limitations, sins, mistakes and betrayals of the members of the Church certainly do affect the very essence of the Church, and particular churches, therefore, are judged not on the basis of their essential churchly life which is expressed in their canonical scriptures, dogmas, sacraments, hierarchical structures and spiritual principles, but rather on the basis of the personalities, practices, and even on the piety and politics of their constituent members—primarily the clergy. Thus the sectarians among the Orthodox call others to join their true ecclesiastical jurisdiction not only when the churches of these others are judged to be formally deficient, incomplete or in error, possessing a human form which is not adequate to God and is therefore not one with the catholic Church, but also when these churches are considered to be of a membership or leadership which is in their opinion only pietistically or politically deficient or erroneous, and even when in these churches the doctrines and canons of the Orthodox Church are officially and formally accepted, although they are challenged or violated by some, and when the sacraments and spiritual life of the Church remain officially in force, although they are misused or abused in practice by some.

The Catholic Fulness

It is the confusion of the *essential mystical existence* of the one, holy, catholic, Orthodox Church—expressed in the integrity of its scriptures, doctrines, sacraments, canons, spirituality and hierarchical structures—with the Church's *actual human membership*—which is always and inevitably limited and sinful—which separates both denominationalists and sectarians from Orthodox Catholic Christians. This is not a new problem. It is one which has plagued the Church from the beginning (syncretism, Montanism), which has flourished with particular power and success in recent centuries, and which is perhaps more dangerous today than ever before because of the manifold frustrations, confusions and passions which oppress the numberless persons and groups, both within and without the Orthodox Church, who have lost the living tradition of the one holy Church of Christ.

The ways of denominationalism and sectarianism are broad and easy. They are broad and easy because they reduce the Church which is not of this world to an institution of this age, thus emptying it of the Cross of catholic wisdom and power. They do this by a clear and consistent use of "earthly logic" which is in direct opposition to the mysteries of the Kingdom of God given to men in Christ and the Spirit. They do this, in a word, by abandoning what is given in the Spirit and by returning to the flesh, as they make of the divine doctrine of the Church a merely "human doctrine" in which the Church is placed under the power of the divisive elemental spirits of this age whose image is passing away.

If the Christian faith will remain for men as God's total and perfect gift of His Kingdom to all men in all times and places, it can only do so through the rediscovery and recovery of the Church in all of its catholic integrity and fulness. Without the practice of traditional catholicity by the members of the Church there may indeed remain believers in Christ who are very inspired and enthusiastic or very well organized and established, but there will no longer remain that divinely called and constituted community of persons which, in every aspect of its personal and corporate existence, lives by the catholic fulness of God's truth and love given in Christ and the Holy Spirit: the one "Church which is His body, the fulness of Him who fills all in all" (Eph. 1:23).

4

Reflections on Eastern Rite Catholicism

My purpose in the few remarks that follow is to try to show what the common Orthodox attitude toward the Eastern Rite movement has been until now, and to raise some questions and offer some guesses concerning the possible role of Eastern Rite Catholicism in future relations between Rome and the Orthodox, especially in the light of the new situation of the whole Christian world. The thoughts expressed are personal intuitions which come from my experiences as a child, a student, a pastor and a teacher all lived deeply within the problematics of the Orthodox-Uniate encounter of the Slav-Americans.

The Common Orthodox Attitude

Our first thoughts in regard to the Eastern Rite question turn to the past, where, for an Orthodox, is found only hatred, bitterness and sin. The very term "Eastern Rite Catholic" or "Uniate" has a bad meaning for an Orthodox. It signifies infidelity and betrayal, not merely the infidelity of the Eastern Rite Catholics to their Orthodox Church, but betrayal by Rome of those children supposedly reunited to their Mother Church in faith and love and on the basis of equality, freedom and inward self-determination. Not only are the Eastern Rite Catholics to be blamed for leaving the true Church, runs the traditional Orthodox argument, but the mistake of their actions has been demonstrated by history, both in their consistent ill-treatment by the Latin Church as well as in their obvious failure to keep their own tradition faithful to its origins and alive to genuinely self-determined development toward the future. This is the common Orthodox view of the "Unia": (1) unfaithful to Orthodoxy, (2) betrayed by Rome, and (3) inwardly impotent to retain and cultivate an authentic self-identity. Virtually every Orthodox statement on Eastern Rite Catholicism carries this three-fold condemnation.

Several years ago, in a publication designed to be read by the average Orthodox Christian, an Orthodox priest wrote an analysis of "the Uniate question" which remains a perfect expression of the common Orthodox attitude. We shall quote long excerpts from this article as the best example of the Orthodox position up to the present moment. After beginning with a brief statement about the ecclesiological self-consciousness of the Roman Church up until its loss of "the concept of one Christian Church inclusive of many Christian traditions" in the tenth century, the author says this about the Union of Brest:

Rome's creation of the Uniate Eastern Catholic Churches at the Union of Brest in 1595 represents not her attempt at an integral unity with Eastern Orthodoxy, but the enactment of her policy to submit to papal authority and to absorb into the Latin Church life all the dissidents outside her immediate fold. No discussions were conducted with the ancient Eastern Patriarchates; rather, an Orthodox splinter group was cunningly subverted and then elevated to represent "the return of the Eastern schismatics." Roman Catholic polemicists have often presented the Unia as an answer to the fervent plea of the dissatisfied Eastern dissidents for a "return" to the tranquil and orderly guidance of the Holy Father, the Pope. In fact, the Uniate Church was born amidst political and economic pressures on an uneducated and poverty-stricken people, it found its base of existence in secrecy, lies, sub-

version, greed, pride, ambition, and false promises—
in all of which Rome herself played no small part.[1]

The author of these words is an American-born and
-educated priest looking at the Eastern Rite question from
the perspective of his studies, especially those of the Byzan-
tine-Roman-Slavic triangle, and of his personal observations
and experiences in the Church. As he continues his analysis
one would think that he would become more positive the
closer that he comes to the happenings of the present day.
But we see that this is not the case:

> Strangely enough, it is the flag of Unia, basically un-
> changed, which the Roman Church still waves before
> the Orthodox every time the subject of unity is raised.
> In our own day Vatican II has restated the case. The
> Council's Decree on the Eastern Catholic Churches
> says: "The Catholic Church holds in high esteem the
> institutions of the Eastern Churches, their liturgical
> rites, ecclesiastical traditions and Christian way of
> life." The decree goes on to urge each individual
> Church and Rite to "retain its traditions whole and
> entire."

> . . . Speaking strictly in terms of the letter of papal
> decrees, statements in support of the integrity of the
> Eastern rites and traditions are nothing new for Rome.
> Since the inception of the Unia of Brest-Litovsk in
> 1595, papal bulls have consistently spoken of the valid-
> ity and praiseworthiness of these rites. In the Bull of
> Union of December 23, 1595, Pope Clement VIII
> clearly granted that all divine offices and sacramental
> administrations be conducted by the "Ruthenians"
> according to the Greek Rite. Despite this support in
> letter, latinizations in the rite in practice began very
> early in the history of the Uniate Church.[2]

[1]Fr. Paul Lazor, "The Uniate Question," *The Orthodox Christian Way*
vol. 7, no. 10 (October, 1967), p. 3.
[2]*Ibid.*, pp. 3-4.

After referring to many examples of the deritualization of the Eastern Rite Catholics and the gradual hybridization of their theology and liturgy, and after indicating that complaints about this are recorded by certain Uniate bishops as early as 1664, the author then tries to demonstrate that the inner mutation of the Eastern Rite Church was not accidental, but essential and inevitable.

This latinizing of the liturgical rites in the Uniate Churches, despite numerous verbal guarantees to the contrary, including Vatican II, is inevitable. Man's faith is expressed in his prayer. Once a man subscribes to the Roman Catholic faith, it is impossible to prevent this way of believing from influencing the manner in which he worships.[3]

And again after offering many examples of how specifically Latin doctrines found their expressions in the Eastern Rite Churches in specifically Latin forms of liturgy and piety unknown to the authentic eastern tradition and therefore not found in "an Orthodox rite," the author concludes:

A man cannot believe and think one way, and then worship according to a rite which expresses another way of believing and thinking. And, precisely, generations of Uniate clergy who have been trained in Roman Catholic schools or in Roman Catholic theology have produced a rite and a form of church life which are so confused and hybridized that, according to the admission of the Uniates themselves, they have simply lost their identity.[4]

And what about the events of the present day?

Today the unity of all Christians in the one Church of Christ is something which is being sincerely sought. Roman Catholicism and Orthodoxy, with their many

[3]*Ibid.*, p. 4.
[4]*Ibid.*, italics his.

centuries of common tradition, and recently-demonstrated attitude of mutual love and respect, have a great possibility of attaining this goal. Yet . . . Rome strangely enough continues to present the way of the Unia. By so doing, she not only promulgates a policy which rings of medieval papalism and which evokes bitter memories of strife between herself and Orthodoxy, but she presents a plan which . . . has failed. If the Uniate Church represents what is in store for the Orthodox who would enter into unity with Rome, then it would be better to lay aside the idea of unity. In addition, through the Unia scheme Rome continues to relegate to a secondary position the real issue, the debate concerning the Faith.[5]

In conclusion—after quoting Fr. Alexander Schmemann's remarks on the Decree on the Eastern Catholic Churches in which he states that for the Orthodox, "the existence of the 'Uniate' Eastern Catholic Churches remains one of the major obstacles to any sincere theological confrontation with the Roman Catholic Church"[6]—the article refers to the success of Photius and Pope John VIII in maintaining the full and perfect unity of the Church in the ninth century, even with the existence of many liturgical differences, "because they had first settled the debate concerning the Faith."[7] And then the final question is raised by the author about the possible role of Eastern Rite Catholics in the future developments of the ecumenical movement, especially if Rome would "abandon the Unia plan" in its relation with the Orthodox Church.

The Uniates in the Future

The attitude presented by this author can be taken as the view of Eastern Rite Catholicism which is to be found in the most enlightened, best-willed circles of the Orthodox Church

[5]*Ibid.*, p. 5, italics his.
[6]Quoted by Fr. Lazor from *The Documents of Vatican II* (Guild Press, New York), p. 387.
[7]Lazor, *loc. cit.*, italics his.

on this question. The task still remains, however, to interpret this attitude on a deeper, spiritual and existential basis, especially in the light of the present happenings in the Christian world, both on the grass-roots level as well as in the formal encounters and official decrees, including those of Pope John Paul II. It is not enough any more for the Orthodox, isolated and alienated from the West, to point to the mutations and frustrations of the Eastern Rite Christians united to Rome and to speak solely in terms of infidelity and betrayal. For although there is a genuine point to this type of attitude, one which in our opinion is fitting and just and which is even being exposed these days by many Eastern Rite Catholics themselves, it is still necessary to go beyond this type of discussion to the more crucial questions of the spiritual meaning of the "Uniate" experience for Eastern Rite Catholics themselves and the ecumenical meaning of this same experience for all Christians who are desiring the perfect unity of all believers in one undivided Church. For, when all is said and done about the events of the past and the situation of the Eastern Rite Catholics today, the only real question is still the question of spirit and truth.

The question may be formulated in this fashion: Can the Eastern Rite Christian find in his church the full possibility of coming to the knowledge of the truth in the most perfect communion with the living God through Christ in the Spirit in the Church? Or, to put the same question in a negative way, are there not formal and essential obstacles which belong to the official spirit and truth of Uniatism which, if pursued to the end, will inevitably lead to a deformed and imperfect experience of the Christian faith? Then, proceding from this fundamental question, there come all of the other questions which are usually given first-line priority in discussions of the Eastern Rite question, namely the problems of cultures, customs, traditions, rituals, mentalities, jurisdictions, obediences, *etc.*, but which now, in view of the fundamental question, are no longer interesting in themselves but solely as relative to the living problems of Christian faith and experience. Taken in this perspective, the questions now become not the superficial ones about "which rite is right" or about the component elements of orientalisms or latinisms in any given church, but about the spiritual meaning of these traditional cultural phenomena for the personal salvation of the believer in God's Kingdom, as well as for the perfectly unified expression of that Kingdom in the ecclesial realities of this world. In the new situation of the world in general, and of the Christian world in particular, do the distinctions of Eastern and Western in general, and of Orthodox and Roman in particular, have any genuine and authentic meaning? Do these terms have real significance in the souls of men? Do believing and striving Christians really think in terms of East and West? In America and Europe especially, do the Orthodox and the Eastern Rite Catholics have some special, traditional, cultural rapport which makes them "closer" and already "more united" than, for example, Latin Rite Catholics and Orthodox? Can there be a realistic discussion of doctrinal and spiritual unity between Rome and Orthodoxy in isolation from the greater, more inclusive unity movements within Christianity as a whole? All of these questions, and the many like them which could be formulated, are crucial to any appreciation of the place of Eastern Rite Catholicism as a presence and a force on the church scene today, and indeed for the days to come.

Loss of Unity

Before we can consider these questions at all and attempt to move toward some answers by stating our personal opinions and unprophetic guesses, we must first bracket the Eastern Rite Catholics as such and consider the wider problem of the whole situation in the Roman and Orthodox churches today. In both of these churches there is a loss of unity of mind and spirit, and a flourishing of opinions and ideas about the direction which the Church must take in the modern world. These conflicts of mind and spirit are not merely between individual members of the churches or between various schools. There are in fact very often conflicts between the official policies of the official churches and the opinions and actions of the Christians at large. There are many examples which could be indicated here. In any case, it is clear that before a fruitful encounter can take place between Rome and Orthodoxy there must be an ordering of one's own house and a discovery of the household's common mind. For the Romans this means primarily the achievement of a spiritually-united post-conciliar church. For the Orthodox it means a self-encounter of brutal honesty and merciless truth, a laying-aside of century-old cliches and empty symbolisms and a coming to grips with the realities of life—and not so much the realities of "others" and the "modern world" as the realities of the real-life situation of contemporary Orthodoxy itself in all of its various dimensions. Although the facts of the Communist and Islamic captivity, with all of the painful by-products of such conditions, makes such a self-encounter almost impossible, there can be no doubt that the fervent desire and the forceful effort to undertake this task will bring the grace and the power of the Spirit to make it possible.

Eastern Rite Catholics—A Bridge?

Until now the Eastern Rite Catholics have been considered by many to play the role of a "bridge" between East and West. Of course these "many" are those of a positive mind since there are the others who would prefer to consider the Uniates as "obstacles" (and lately even the metaphor of "door-mat" has been suggested!). But in the world today where these historical labels of East and West seem to mean less and less, and where they may even already signify totally obsolete concepts with little or no practical and concrete application in life, the idea of a "bridge" and even of an "obstacle" (not to mention a "door-mat") becomes meaningless. As we look at the present events in the Christian world, the descriptions of "Eastern" and "Western" are indeed very questionable, not merely because the world is growing smaller and cultural barriers in general are falling, but because the institutions themselves which formally hold these titles as modifying adjectives do not really require them to reflect any reality in fact. We can find many Western churches, for example, adopting and implementing forms and practices which have been traditionally understood as being exclusively Eastern; and on the hand, we can find forms and practices in the traditional Eastern churches which are clearly not the common property of East and West but rather direct borrowings from post-schism Western sources—and this includes Orthodox churches not united to Rome. To be very concrete, when we can find a Benedictine monastery, not of the Eastern Rite, with a theological, liturgical and spiritual style of life which is more Orthodox, judged by strictly Orthodox standards, than certain churches which are canonically and jurisdictionally Orthodox in union with the Eastern patriarchs, such as certain former Uniate Slav parishes, and which is even more Eastern in its life than many formally Eastern Rite churches, then we must radically reconsider the whole debate and admit that the official labels of East and West, and even of Roman and Orthodox, must be seriously questioned if not simply discarded as being formal at best, when they are not plainly false. This type of argument can be carried over into other areas of church life where similar examples are possible, such as in theology by comparing the scholastic manuals of the Orthodox and Eastern Rite Catholics with the patristic teachings of certain Westerners; or the political ideas of Greece and Spain in contrast to the political ideas of many American Christians of all churchly backgrounds; or the various approaches to the ecumenical movement, each of which can find its complement in any other church or denomination. Indeed in such a situation, where the significations of East and West are being emptied of their meaning in theory and in fact, the very idea of the Eastern Rite as "bridge" or as "obstacle" becomes proportionately devoid of serious application.

The Real Question

In our opinion, therefore, the only conclusion can be that, given the continued growing together of the entire Christian world, with increased mutual borrowings and progressive disregard and disinterest in one's own past as something valuable in itself, Eastern Rite Catholicism as a particular institution will be really negligible. The Uniates will be lost in the stream of events because the questions of cultures and customs and rituals and traditions and jurisdictions and authorities will be simply not interesting. Man in search for the Living God and the unity of all men in Him, in spirit and in truth, will care less about the preservation or the propagation of the "mentality" of one's past. No one will care about celibacy or vestments or altar bells as such; and not even about papal infallibilty and the Immaculate Conception and *filioque* as problems of custom and tradition. All of these questions will be subordinated to the ultimate question of truth, as rightly and justly they must be. And the real question will finally be asked: "What do you think of Christ, whose son is He?" And everyone must answer, seeking the truth in terms of everything that one can know and appreciate regardless of its historical and cultural origin, and in the uninhibited confirmation and adoption of "whatever is true, whatever is honorable, whatever is just, whatever is pure, whatever is lovely, whatever is gracious" (Phil. 4:8). Out of all this will come the discovery of the unity of all people in God, in spirit and in truth.

Some may think that this is unrealistic and utopian, and that the realistic and concrete truth is that men are in fact still profoundly determined by their past and their culture, and that these elements must still be considered as playing a dominant role in decisions of ultimate concern. But for all the importance of various traditions in the life of a person, still the facts which we referred to above already show, in our opinion, that what one person may consider as utopian or a thing of the future is indeed already becoming the situation today. There is no doubt that if we would take as examples not only theologians and professional churchmen but also ordinary people in the pews, we would find that the distinctions among them on questions of doctrine, practice and policy of Christian faith are not made as easily according to churchly distinctions as according to the individual persons in question. It is just a matter of plain fact that certain Latin

Catholics, Eastern Rite Catholics, Orthodox and Protestants find themselves more united on certain questions with each other than with members of their own churchly institutions. And these questions are often not merely accidental and non-essential questions concerning secondary matters of small significance. These are indeed questions of ultimate importance: questions about the understanding and experience of God, man, the Church and the world.

In such a situation, which in our opinion is already here, Eastern Rite Catholics will have no particular task but to do what all believers must do, namely to strive to find their place individually and as a group among those men whom the Lord desires to be saved and to come to the knowledge of the truth. In doing this, however, Eastern Rite Catholics, as all people who desire life with God through Christ and the Spirit, must resist the temptation to be defenders of rituals and mentalities and jurisdictions. They must not regard questions of cultural purity and formal authority as questions of prime importance. They must realize that to strive in this direction is a vain striving, a striving after the wind. They must realize that for a Christian to give his soul in return for a whole world of traditional rituals or cultural mentalities or external validities is in fact to lose his soul; and only the one who is truly willing to lose these things will gain life in the end. And when these worlds are understood in such a formal and artificial way that they are even spoken of almost as sorts of "vestments" which can be put on and off at will, and even then for the most dubious reasons which range from a lust for narcissistic self-affirmation to an outright hatred and spite for others, then we have already entered the realm of foolishness and fantasy, not to say sickness and sin and death of the spirit.

Christians of all churches are tempted thus to lose their lives by the desire to keep the Christian faith wrapped up solely in these terms: Eastern Rite Catholics who defend their existence solely in these terms; the Latins who force them to do so by posing the problem of multiple rites in the Roman communion solely in these terms; and the Orthodox who would formulate their criticism, as well as the case for their own supposed integrity, solely in these terms.

A Unity of Faith and Life

This brings us back to the original point raised in the article quoted at the beginning of our present remarks. The only just reason for the Orthodox to stay out of union with Rome can be a reason of faith and doctrine, not one of culture, ritual, tradition, mentality or jurisdiction. For even if the Orthodox could admit in theory what has never existed in fact, namely that an Eastern church could remain inwardly untouched while being in union with Rome, that it could retain its cultural integrity and develop and cultivate all of its ancient and unique customs and traditions without fear of repression or adverse influence—even then, in such supposedly acceptable conditions, the Orthodox still could not enter into such a union as long as it would fail to see in Rome a faith and life perfectly compatible with its own. The fact that the faith and life of Rome would not be forced upon them would not be sufficient reason for the Orthodox to have union with Rome. For the Roman experience, albeit exclusively for the Romans, must still be one which is seen by the Orthodox to be perfectly "true, honorable, just, pure, lovely and gracious" for full union to be meaningful, honest, and capable of bearing fruit. Until now the Orthodox claim that this is not the case—that they do not see such a compatible Christianity in the Roman Church. Thus they refuse to admit, as the Eastern Rite Catholics are willing to admit, that Latin Christianity is all right for the Latins but not all right for the Orientals. Unlike the Uniates, the Orthodox say that certain elements in Latin Christianity are not all right for anyone, including the Latins, and that the question of the ritual integrity of the Eastern Rite Catholics is not the real question at all. The real question concerns the unacceptable elements which the Orthodox hope will be seen by all who seek the unity of the faith and rejected by all not in terms of cultural mentality but in terms of spirit and truth.

Thus the great hope of the present is not to be found in the so-called "purification" of the Eastern Rites or in any privileged "autonomy" or "independence" for "Oriental churches" which accept some sort of Vatican connection, however limited and carefully formulated. The great hope lies rather in the common discovery of one faith, one Lord, one baptism, one God and Father of us all. And the situation at present seems capable of feeding that hope more than the centuries of union councils and decrees. For in the cataclysmic events of this present era we have the freedom to exercise the divine command to seek the Kingdom of God and His righteousness, by forgetting what lies behind and stretching forward to what lies ahead, in the perfect assurance that all shall be ours as well—including the assurance that all who believe, pray and work in His name will be truly one as He and His Father are one.

. . . .

5

Children and Holy Communion

The Orthodox Church over the centuries has consistently followed the practice of allowing baptized and chrismated children, including infants in arms, to participate in holy communion. This practice was originally not an exclusively "Eastern" one. There is ample evidence indicating that baptized children were brought to the altar for holy communion in the early Western Church as well. The cessation of this practice in the Middle Ages may be attributed to the clericalization of the Church, the withdrawal of the eucharist generally from lay people (with the complete withdrawal of the chalice), and the triumph of a decadent scholastic theology.[1] This Western medieval practice of forbidding baptized children to participate in the eucharist was retained with almost no exception in the Protestant churches. It was also adopted by the later Uniate Eastern churches and also affected certain areas of the Orthodox Church where communion was administered to children before their first confession only in the form of the consecrated wine, if it was not withdrawn altogether.

---

[1] On this point see the paper of Dr. David Holeton, an Anglican scholar from Canada, presented at a conference on "Eucharist With Children," held in 1980 in Bad Segeberg, Germany. The conference was sponsored by the Faith and Order Commission and the Office of Education of the World Council of Churches, together with the Evangelical Academy of North Elbia. Virtually all aspects of the issue were discussed. Papers from the conference are available from the WCC, P.O. Box 66, 150 route de Ferney, 1211 Geneva 20, Switzerland. Among the papers is a keynote address by Fr. Cyrille Argenti, a Greek Orthodox priest from France, describing the Orthodox position.

The Baptism of Children

The traditional Orthodox teaching is that baptism and chrismation are always immediately fulfilled in the reception of holy communion. When children are baptized and chrismated, they must be communed as well.

In the Orthodox view, children can and must be baptized if there are adult members of the Church, usually but not necessarily their parents, who will see that they are raised and nurtured in the faith and life of the Church. If there are no adults to care for the children's spiritual life and churchly upbringing, then it is normally understood by the Orthodox that such children ought not be baptized.

Baptism is not magic. It is not an act in which something happens to a person in isolation from the ongoing life of the Church into which the person is born in the baptismal mystery. The Orthodox Church has never taught (except in some westernized catechisms) that persons who have not been sacramentally baptized cannot enter into the Kingdom of God. Nor has it been the teaching that unbaptized "innocents," particularly children, can have only "natural" and not "supernatural" happiness after death. What happens ultimately to the sacramentally unbaptized, as to the baptized, is known to God alone who sees and judges every life. God decides each person's eternal destiny, according to His gracious providence, justly and mercifully, in ways known to Himself.

Christians who practice their faith and participate in the sacramental life of the Church will baptize the children in their care so that they may be delivered from the power of sin, death and the devil which reigns in this fallen world. Christians baptize their children in order to bring them into the gracious life of the Church, which is the Kingdom of God on earth. They baptize their children and feed them with the Bread of Christ the Savior, so that from their earliest days they may be in communion with the Lord and live by His grace and power, and not by the graceless forces of evil which abound in the world.

The only reason for faithful and responsible adults not to baptize the children in their care, according to Orthodoxy, and so to have them sealed with God's Holy Spirit and communed with the eucharistic gifts, is the fear that the baptized children might be gravely tempted to abandon the faith and to defile the sacramental mysteries. This was the case in the past, as for example in the lives of Ss. Basil and Ambrose, who were not brought into the sacramental life of the Church by their holy parents who feared that they might sin after participating in the Church's holy mysteries and be left excommunicated for many years, perhaps even to their deathbed, for returning to the mire after once having been cleansed (see 2 Pet. 2:22). Such was the extreme sensitivity to the sacredness of the sacraments in the early Church. We have so lost this sensitivity today that we can hardly understand and appreciate such an attitude. Be that as it may, however, the positive teaching remains: When children will be properly cared for in the Church, and when there is no special fear that they will be forced into apostasy, they can and must be brought to baptism, chrismation and holy communion from infancy so that they can grow and develop in the light and truth of Christ, by the grace and power of the Holy Spirit, from their earliest days.

Baptism and Communion

Most Christians agree that children may be baptized. Those who do not (Baptists, Disciples of Christ, and others) claim that they cannot because they are unable to fulfill the condition for baptism, which is to make a free and voluntary confession and commitment of faith in Christ. Those who are opposed to the baptism of children, particularly infants, generally agree, however, that if children are baptized, it is only logical that they be invited to the Lord's Supper as well. They use this argument against those Christian groups which baptize children but forbid them to participate in holy communion. Their argument on this point, according to the Orthodox, is convincing. What the Orthodox do not agree with, however, is not only that children should be forbidden baptism and communion, as these people argue; but that communion may be used as a means of fostering the desire for baptism, as is sometimes being done now in these denominations where unbaptized children are invited to participate in the Lord's Supper as served in these churches. This, in the Orthodox view, is totally unacceptable. It indicates a complete misunderstanding of both baptism and holy communion.

The overwhelming majority of Christians in the Roman and Reformed churches (Roman Catholics, Eastern Rite Catholics, Episcopalians, Lutherans, Presbyterians, Methodists . . .) practice infant baptism while forbidding baptized infants and small children to have holy communion as it is celebrated in their churches. These people generally hold that infants may, and even must, be baptized because of the faith of the community, particularly their families, but cannot receive holy communion because communion, unlike baptism, requires a personal act of discernment, faith and penitence on the part of the communicant which the infant and small child cannot make. They argue that communion requires some sort of understanding and commitment which baptism does not. Why this is so is not clear to the Orthodox, nor to those denominations mentioned above who practice what they call "believer's baptism," that is, baptism only for those capable of making some sort of confession and commitment.

Those who practice infant baptism but not infant communion usually answer objections to their practice by insisting that baptism and communion are two different sacraments, or rites, and as such have different purposes with different conditions necessary to fulfill those purposes. Those with a "high" sacramental view generally say that baptism is to wash away the stain and guilt of original sin and to allow a person to enter God's Kingdom and to have supernatural happiness after death. Those who do not have such a "high" sacramental view say generally that baptism is a service of dedication to God and association with the Christian community. Both approaches agree, however, that participation in holy communion, whether understood by those of the "high" view as the "real" body and blood of Christ or by the others as a "symbolic" memorial meal, requires some act of conscious discernment and desire on the part of the communicant which baptism does not. To be sure, many would acknowledge that small children can make some sort of action recognizing communion, even if it is in a childish way, and that this would be sufficient for their inclusion in the eucharist meal, however any given denomination understands it. What virtually no one except the Orthodox accepts is that baptism always and necessarily implies immediate participation in the holy eucharist; that there are not two different sets of purposes and conditions for participation in these acts in separate and isolated ways; that they belong together essentially; and that infants and small children participate fully in the sacramental life of the Church through their sponsoring adults, and develop their faith, understanding, commitment and desire to participate in the Church as they personally and naturally grow and mature through the years.

In the Orthodox view, a human being who will be baptized, chrismated and communed in the Church must meet certain conditions which make the sacramental acts meaningful and real. For infants and very small children, these conditions are virtually limited to having caring adults whose spiritual lives they share. As the children grow, the conditions for sacramental participation change according to their maturity and ability. Personal faith becomes necessary. Understanding is required. Free and voluntary commitment must be offered. A sense of sin and repentance must be revealed. A firm intention to follow Christian theological and ethical teachings must be realized. But exactly how these conditions, and any others, are actually required and fulfilled differs greatly from person to person. What an infant has to do is different from what his adult guardians have to do. What a senile old person has to understand and profess is not the same as that of a young person at the height of his or her spiritual powers and energies. Conditions for sacramental participation in the Church differ between the intelligent and the retarded, the neophytes and the mature, the young and the old, the strong and the weak. This is just a matter of common sense, which, it might be mentioned, is never opposed to Christian teachings. What is required of children in regard to their participation in the sacramental life of the Church is governed by their adult guardians, parents and pastors. In the case of adults, the final word belongs to their spiritual fathers, pastors and bishops. But to baptize anyone, according to the Orthodox understanding, without chrismation and holy communion following immediately is like being born without living. It is like having Pascha without Pentecost and the subsequent life of the Kingdom of God.

Chrismation and Communion

Further questions arise in regard to holy communion and children (and also adults) when the sacrament of chrismation is considered. Traditionally only the Orthodox and the Eastern Rite Roman Catholics chrismate infants at the time of baptism. Most other Christians have as a "counterpart" to the Orthodox "chrismation" the sacrament or rite of "confirmation." This is understood differently in different denominations, but in all of these groups it is generally administered separately from baptism and at a later age.

In relation to holy communion, some of the churches which have confirmation apart from baptism (like the traditional Roman Catholics) administer the confirmation after holy communion, *i.e.*, they offer communion first, at an age considered appropriate, and then they have confirmation later. Generally the age for first communion is seven or eight, with sometime after twelve for confirmation. Other groups (like the Lutherans) insist that confirmation must preceed holy communion, and they do not allow unconfirmed persons to partake in their services of the Lord's Supper. In these churches a person's first communion is generally rather late in life, often coming only in one's teens.

Although the Orthodox disagree with virtually all of the Western Christian confessions about the meaning of "chrismation" or "confirmation," the Orthodox firmly agree with those who insist that confirmation should precede participation in holy communion, however it is understood. This is the traditional order in the apostolic and patristic Church, the only order which is sensible to the Orthodox who believe that chrismation is the person's personal reception of the gift of the Holy Spirit after being born anew in baptism; the person's personal pentecost after dying and rising with Christ in His holy pascha. As the Spirit's coming fulfills the resurrection and glorification of Jesus and ushers in the Kingdom of God, so, in the Orthodox view, chrismation follows baptism and leads to participation in the holy eucharist, the mystical banquet of God's unending Kingdom. According to the Orthodox understanding and experience, "confirmation" after participation in holy communion is inconceivable, unless, of course, it is understood not as the Holy Spirit "confirming" and "sealing" the faith of the newly-baptized, but as the individual "confirming" and "sealing" his own faith as an adult, which, in any case, is not the Orthodox position nor, the Orthodox would argue, that of the apostolic Church of the first centuries.

Children are Invited

In the Orthodox Church, baptized and chrismated children are invited to participate in the liturgical celebration of the holy eucharist because they are members of Christ's body, the Church. As children were members of the old covenant church and participated fully in its liturgical life (being offered in the temple, circumcised, eating the passover meal, *etc.*) so children are members of God's new and final covenant in His Son Jesus through the sacramental mysteries. They are redeemed, saved, forgiven, accepted and integrated into the new covenant community by the mysteries of baptism, chrismation and the holy eucharist.

According to the scriptures as traditionally interpreted by the Orthodox, Jesus Himself willed the inclusion of children into the saving life of His Church. He is found on the pages of the evangelical writings rebuking His disciples with great indignation for forbidding the children to come to Him.

And they were bringing children to Him, that He
might touch them; and the disciples rebuked them.
But when Jesus saw it he was indignant, and said to
them, "Let the children come to me and do not hinder
them; for to such belongs the Kingdom of God.
Truly, I say to you, whoever does not receive the
Kingdom of God like a child shall not enter it." And
He took them in His arms and blessed them, laying
His hands on them (Mark 10:14-16; also Matt.
18:3, 19:13-15; Luke 18:15-17).

Judging from the conference recently held on the subject
in Bad Segeberg, many theologians, pastors, parents and
teachers in both Roman Catholic and Reformed churches are
now interpreting these words of Jesus as teaching that small
children should be allowed to participate in the Lord's Supper. Most of those who are of this mind, however, are not
yet prepared to open holy communion in their respective
denominations to infants in arms. They still contend that
some sort of conscious willingness and understanding, however slight, must be present in children to warrant their
participation in the holy meal, however it is understood. They
are in favor, by and large, of drastically lowering the age for
participation, and minimizing the conditions, especially those
having to do with understanding, which more often than not,
they agree, amounts in practice to the child's (and even the
adult's) ability to answer certain questions verbally, and to
repeat certain phrases in an external manner, without genuine
comprehension and conviction. They also appear to be generally opposed to the churches having special services of holy
communion for children (although the Roman Catholic
Church seems officially to favor "children's masses"), with
their main intention and desire being the inclusion of children
into the eucharistic gatherings of the churches as such. The
title of the Bad Segeberg conference, "Eucharist With Children," illustrates this concern clearly, which is not simply to
allow children to "make their communion" at an earlier age,
but specifically to have children partake with all of the members of the church gathered to the Lord's Supper as full mem-

bers of the church in their own right. It should be mentioned, too, that the issue of "children's rights" plays no small role in the movement for children's communion in the minds and hearts of many of its advocates, especially in the Protestant churches.

The Orthodox Today

While happily greeting the movement for greater participation of younger children in holy communion in the various Christian churches and denominations, the thoughtful Orthodox must still wonder at some of its aspects. The main concern, in summary, is whether or not the movement is generally being conducted for the right reasons; not only the right reasons about the meaning of the Church and the sacraments, but the right reasons about children as well. A new and different attitude and practice in the Roman Catholic and Reformed churches on this issue indicates a new and different rationale from times past. It evokes a new and different theological vision and experience. The fact that most of the advocates of greater participation in holy communion for small children are not ready to defend the propriety of infant communion, and do not see the essential interconnectedness and order between baptism, chrismation and the eucharist seen by the Orthodox, indicates that this new rationale, whatever it is and whatever its cause and inspiration—theological, liturgical, ecumenical, pedagogical, sociological, psychological, political—,is not that of the Orthodox Church nor, in the Orthodox view, that of the orthodox-catholic tradition of the first millenium of the Church in East and West. Be that as it may, however, the present movement, whatever its causes, motivations and goals, presents a serious and significant challenge to the Orthodox themselves.

In the various Orthodox churches today, especially in America, there are any number of malpractices in regard to the sacraments generally, the eucharist in particular, and the communion of children most specifically. In many churches which have recently (and not so recently) been converted from

Uniatism, children are still being barred from receiving holy communion after baptism and chrismation until they have their first confession, not seldomly after a preparation which is customary and formal. A young mother who was refused holy communion for her newly-baptized infants in one such parish remarked: "And I thought the only differences between the various Orthodox churches were cultural and ethnic; I see now that there are real differences in faith as well." The woman was right. To forbid the eucharist to baptized-chrismated infants is not simply a matter of discipline, custom or tradition. It is a matter of faith. Those who practice such a faith within the Orthodox Church are clearly heretical since they willfully divide the Church by consciously violating her official doctrine by their personal and arbitrary choice and opinion.

There are also communities and parishes in the Orthodox Church which have been influenced by post-Reformation Latin theology in which infants and small children are given only the consecrated wine at the Divine Liturgy until they make their first confession. In these places infants and small children are also forbidden to receive holy communion at the Church's liturgy of the presanctified gifts. According to traditional Orthodox theology, there is no justification for such practices. They have their roots in decadent scholasticized theology, being defended by such far-fetched arguments as the one which points out that in the Holy Scriptures Jesus said "all of you" only in reference to the drinking of His Blood, and not the eating of His Body, while St. Paul, in his first letter to the Corinthians, insists that all communicants must "discern the Lord's body" but says nothing about His blood. Thus the conclusion is drawn that infants and small children who cannot "discern the Lord's body" are still part of the "all of you" of the Church and as such may be given the consecrated wine from the chalice until they are able to confess their sins and recognize clearly that the bread of the altar is truly the body of Christ!

There is also the practice in many Orthodox churches that infants and small children are brought to holy communion while the rest of the congregation, including the adults who bring them to the altar, refrain from partaking of the sacraments. There is also the practice that infants and small children who are brought regularly to holy communion before their first confession cease their regular participation at that time and begin, with the other adults in the churches, to come only a few times a year. There are also churches where the children's approach to confession and communion is a mere formality, devoid of authentic spiritual understanding and commitment. And there are places where the children, with the adults, approach confession and holy communion with anxiety and fear, and without the solemn and yet joyful sense of being forgiven and united in communion with the merciful Lord. In still other places, sacramental confession is not practiced at all, by children or adults, who even sometimes consider it as "Roman Catholic" and not Orthodox! There are even instances in some churches where confession and communion are forced upon children (and even adults) when they have done something especially bad, with the participation in the sacraments being a part of their "punishment." All of these malpractices indicate terrible misunderstanding and misuse of the sacraments of the Church. They show that in many instances sacramental participation for children and adults has little or nothing to do with Christ and the Christian life as such.

The movement for greater involvement of small children in holy communion now stirring in the Roman Catholic and Reformed churches can be a great blessing from God for many people. It can be an especially great blessing for the Orthodox if it forces the adult members of the Orthodox churches, particularly the bishops and priests, to examine, correct and deepen their own commitment to the Orthodox faith and to the sacramental teachings and practices of the Church as provided by the Lord Himself, which were taught and practiced everywhere by His apostles and saints. The issue of children and holy communion is one more critical challenge confronting the Orthodox in the modern world.

The Traditional Practice

Children are initiated into the mysteries of Christ in the Orthodox Church about the fortieth day after their birth. At that time they are presented to the Lord in the churchly temple. They are greeted by the priest and people at their entrance into the community with prayer, blessing, exorcism and anointing. Their adult sponsors reject the devil in their name and accept Christ on their behalf, reciting the Church's symbol of faith, the Nicene-Constantinopolitan creed. The infants are immersed three times in water sanctified for their baptism in the name of the Holy Trinity. They are clothed in white robes. Crosses are placed around their necks. And their death and resurrection in the baptismal waters is confirmed by a second anointing, this time with chrism consecrated by the Church's bishops which is applied to all parts of their bodies as "the seal of the gift of the Holy Spirit."

After their baptism and chrismation the children are carried in triple procession around the baptismal font which, in the words of St. Cyril of Jerusalem, is the tomb in which they have died to this world and the womb in which they have been reborn into the renewed world of the Kingdom of God mystically present on earth in the Church of the Messiah. Their entrance into everlasting life is accompanied with the chanting of the apostolic proclamation: "As many as have been baptised into Christ have put on Christ. Alleluia!"[2]

After the reading of the Word of God, the children are brought to the altar table to partake of the holy eucharist which they continue to receive at each celebration of the mystical supper, particularly on the Lord's Day, as they grow up as members of the Church. Their manner of participation is the same as that of the adults. A piece of the consecrated bread is taken on a spoon with the sanctified wine and is placed by the celebrant or the deacon into the communicant's

[2]See Alexander Schmemann, *Of Water and the Spirit: A Liturgical Study of Baptism* (Crestwood, N.Y., St. Vladimir's Seminary Press, 1974) for a complete commentary on the rites of baptism and chrismation with their relationship to the eucharist.

mouth. In the case of infants the portion of the Lord's body is obviously very small. Thus the children become members of the Church which is Christ's body by participating in the marriage supper of the Lamb together with all others who have been blessed to eat bread in the Kingdom of God. Their personal passover in baptism has been sealed by their personal pentecost in chrismation, and they enter personally into God's Kingdom by sharing in the eucharistic sacrifice of Christ in the Church.

Spiritual Growth

Small children certainly know that something is happening around them and to them in the eucharistic worship of the church, particularly in their participation in holy communion. They know this as much as they know that something happens at home when they are carried, kissed and fed. Infants have minds as well as sensations and feelings. Their minds develop as they grow, interpreting and evaluating their sensible and emotional experiences.

Before they are even a year old, children begin to recognize when they are in church. They begin to participate in the corporate liturgical worship and to receive the sacraments with the first signs of conscious awareness and understanding. They express a yearning for the chalice when it is presented to them. They open their mouths to receive holy communion. They relate to the chalice, the cross and the icons with infantile recognition and veneration. They learn to kiss the holy things as they learn to kiss their family and friends. As they grow older, their recognition and understanding increases, and normally their participation in liturgical worship becomes more eager and enthusiastic. They look forward to lighting candles and kissing icons and receiving the eucharistic gifts. When they see the priests and the chalice they express their excitement. They make noises and reach out and open their mouths. They recognize certain songs, especially the "Alleluia," and "Lord, have mercy" and the "Holy God." They move their hands to make the sign of the cross. They enjoy all of the activity. The process is organic and natural. It happens just like all other things happen in their lives. And, like all other things, it requires adult assistance and care in order to happen properly and well, with understanding and commitment.

Adult Assistance

The greatest assistance which adults can offer children in their spiritual life is to provide them with a sane and joyful environment in which to ripen and develop. Children are tribal. They do what their community does, and that depends on adults. They imitate their elders and peers. And they form themselves mentally and spiritually within the conditions available to them in their everyday life. It is not enough, for example, for children to be loved by others. They must also experience others (particularly their parents and family members) loving each other. The greatest gift that adults can give children is the gift of living with people who love and trust each other so that the children can enter into and learn from this love. This is what should happen in the churchly community, particularly at the eucharistic assembly. Children learn how to worship in a worshipping community. They must be an organic part of that community in order to learn. If the children are excluded from worshipping and communing with adults (again particularly their parents), or if the adult community into which they are integrated is worshipping wrongly or poorly or not at all, then the children are, to say the least, at a tremendous disadvantage.

In addition to providing a truly worshipping community in which children can grow and develop, adults who care for children in the Church must consciously nourish and cultivate the children's awareness and understanding. Children must be brought into the liturgical assembly with continuous preparation. The liturgy itself must be prepared. The adults who lead and participate in it must be prepared. And the children must be prepared.

The preparation of children for liturgical worship is basically a teaching activity conducted in conjunction with the children's actual liturgical experiences.[3] Adults have to talk with children about the Lord and His liturgy. Children generally love to talk, and they certainly love talking about Christ and the Church when they have experiences to share with adults who welcome and encourage such conversation. Adults who live with children must be especially encouraged and aided in talking with their children on spiritual and liturgical themes in an honest, open and natural way, without fear or anxiety of any kind. This is why the education and spiritual direction of adults in the Church is the first and best means of helping children to grow fruitfully in the faith. No amount of formal catechetical classes in church schools can replace spontaneous conversation between children and informed and committed adults whose lives are shaped and inspired by liturgical worship and eucharistic communion. Indeed, formal classes may actually prove harmful to students deprived of this privilege.[4]

Talking with children about God and the Church is usually based on Bible stories, lives of saints and events in church history, done without moralizing, "making points," or forcing the children to "tell what it means to them." The assisting adults should show how these stories, persons and events, with their familiar characters and happenings, are read, sung about, depicted in icons and solemnly celebrated at the Church's liturgical worship. This means, for the most part, that the adults simply point out to the children what to watch for in the liturgical readings, hymns, icons and rituals.

Children love more than anything to know what is going on. They love to recognize what is happening. They enjoy suspense and anticipation. They delight in waiting for something to occur, and then to see it happening just as they knew it would. This is why they love to read the same books and sing the same songs and play the same games again and again. And this is why, if they are allowed to participate in

[3]See Sophie Koulomzin, *Our Church and Our Children* (St. Vladimir's Seminary Press, Crestwood, N.Y., 1976).

[4]This point was pressed in an "Open Letter to the Churches" published by the Orthodox Christian Education Commission in America in May, 1968. See *Orthodox America, 1794-1976* (Syosset, N.Y., Orthodox Church in America, 1975), p. 238.

the Church's liturgical worship and are aided in doing so by sharing with adults, they will love to participate and there will be little need to compel them.

Moral and Spiritual Development

In addition to the intellectual and informational aspects of preparing children for liturgical and eucharistic worship, there are spiritual and moral aspects as well. This part of the preparation, at least in the beginning with small children, has to do with external behavior. To participate fruitfully in eucharistic worship a certain external and formal discipline must be observed so that the deeper, internal spiritual experiences may take place. This means that children must learn how to stand in church, how to pay attention, how not to bother others, *etc.* It also means that they must be trained in certain ascetical exercises in preparation for holy communion, as they are able, according to their age and maturity. These "ascetical exercises" include such things as praying personally and fasting as one can; dressing in a manner proper to liturgical celebration with others, particularly adults; confessing one's sins in a formal sacramental manner when the time comes when this is possible and necessary; asking forgiveness for one's sins and faults; making acts of reparation and reconciliation, *etc.* In the spiritual life the practitioner first learns the letter of the law before he or she can enter into the glorious liberty of gracious communion with the Lord. This biblical principle certainly applies to the preparation of children (and adults) for eucharistic worship.

As children grow they must be helped to interiorize their liturgical and sacramental experiences, to apply the events of the liturgy to themselves, and to take responsibility for their participation, especially as it applies to their daily lives. This, in a word, is what spiritual growth is all about: the progressive actualization in everyday living of that which one experiences sacramentally in the liturgical, eucharistic assembly. One of the essential aspects of this growth which begins early in life is the ability of persons to undergo temptation and trial;

to take responsibilty for their thoughts, words and deeds; and to relate properly to their feelings and emotions, especially those of a negative character which are not directly dependent upon their voluntary and conscious decisions and actions.

Among the worst things that adults can do to children is to tell them how they ought to *feel,* especially in regard to liturgical worship and sacramental communion. Feelings are not in a person's control. People feel how they feel; and that depends on numberless factors most of which are beyond their decisions and desires. God does not command feelings. He rather teaches His people how they ought to think and act in relation to their emotions. In a word, the Lord does not command feelings but tells His servants what they ought to do about them in regard to themselves, to the others with whom they live, and to God Himself.

As children grow in understanding and in spiritual and moral awareness, they inevitably grow in the awareness of their weaknesses and faults. They have trouble sorting things out, clarifying their ideas, handling their feelings, resisting their temptations, and generally in understanding and accepting what is happening in and around them in many ways. Children must be helped with these difficulties at an early age. The liturgy, which in certain cases may doubtlessly be the cause of their troubles, is nevertheless essential in aiding children in their spiritual growth not only as it offers a vision and calls for a committed action, but also as it comforts and encourages in its revelation of God who commands and judges as He also protects, forgives, encourages, inspires, enlightens and restores.

Sacramental Confession

At the proper time, which is different for every person, children participating in eucharistic worship must consciously begin to take responsibility for their lives, particularly their sins. They do this by sacramental confession before God and their fellow creatures in the presence of their priest. Sacramental confession, which is neither a legal tribunal nor a psychological counselling session, is necessary in order for the struggling child of God, of whatever age, to have the assurance of the Lord's mercy and forgiveness as well as the opportunity to see himself clearly in God's light and to receive assistance in carrying on the spiritual struggle which faith in the Lord and participation in His eucharistic sacrifice demand. Both the ability to acknowledge one's sins openly before others and the not seldomly more difficult ability to accept forgiveness and reconciliation is essential to the spiritual life of a person. It must begin in childhood, at the proper moment, organically, naturally and without a fuss.[5]

Remembrance and Return

As children grow in understanding and awareness, both intellectually and spiritually, they may turn away from eucharistic participation in the Church. This can happen for any number of reasons. At the youngest age it can happen simply because of fear, shyness or embarrassment. This is usually the case when something unpleasant happens to the child in church, not seldomly involving some bad or unwise behavior on the part of the adult members of the community, including the clergy. When such things occur it is imperative not to force the child to participate in holy communion while at the same time not withdrawing the child from the liturgical assembly. Children who have an unfortunate experience in church must be kept in the liturgical gathering, being encouraged gently and firmly to participate when they are ready to do so with the proper use of the freedom available to them at their particular stage of spiritual development.

Older children may withdraw from communion because of intellectual and moral confusion and misunderstanding. Withdrawal can also occur when older children are unable to relate properly to their frustrations, doubts, weaknesses and failures. And some young people may leave the eucharistic community simply because they reject what it stands for and

[5]See *We Return to God* and *If We Confess our Sins,* published by the Department of Religious Education of the Orthodox Church in America.

reveals, preferring other ways of thinking and acting. It is important to realize that children go through stages of rejection and return as a necessary and providential part of their spiritual maturation which leads to their perfection and ultimate salvation. Adults go through these stages as well. In dealing with young people at such times, and especially children, is it necessary to understand what is happening but never to justify it by any form of rationalization or condescension. The adults must remain firm and committed, practicing what they believe and know, testifying to it with love and compassion so that the younger members will have strong and steadfast examples against which to test and refine their own thought and actions. Hopefully most cases of rejection, which happen at different times for different reasons, will prove themselves to be temporary and passing. It is exactly at such times of struggle that early childhood experiences prove their critical significance and value.[6]

Persons who from their earliest days have had the experience of liturgical worship and eucharistic communion in the Church have something to remember and return to throughout their lives. The "house of the Father" with its open doors, its shining robes, its festive music and its table prepared for the celebration of their homecoming exists for them. It is a part of their lives which has to be dealt with and cannot be denied. Happy are they who have such an experience to contend with. Truly blessed are they who have been fed with the Bread of Life from infancy by those for whom the eucharistic sacrifice of the Church's divine liturgy constitutes the source, the goal and the very heart of their existence on earth.

[6]This point is made in the writings of Fyodor Dostoevsky, especially in *The Brothers Karamazov.*

6

Orthodox Christianity
and the American Spirit

Through my experience as an American-born and -educated pastor and teacher in the Orthodox Church in America, I am convinced that Will Herberg is correct in his basic conclusions about religion in America and American religion.[1] I believe as well that Robert Bellah's observations about the existence of an American "civil religion" are fundamentally sound.[2] Americans are supposed to be Protestants, Catholics and Jews, with each of these "major faiths" preserving the peculiarities of its respective customs and traditions for the private enjoyment of its members—more and more on the members' own terms and in the ways that they individually desire—while they profess and defend the "common faith" of the "American way of life." For the majority of Eastern Orthodox Americans, this has meant that, since they also are true Americans who contribute to the nation's progress and give loyal support to the nation's values and goals (not seldom through the sacrificial shedding of blood), they too deserve "recognition" as a "major religion," indeed as the nation's "fourth major faith."

The point not only is that members of the Orthodox churches, both lay people and clergy, have accepted the

---

[1] Will Herberg, *Protestant, Catholic, Jew* (Anchor Books, 1960), especially chapter 5, "The Religion of Americans and American Religion."

[2] Robert N. Bellah, "Civil Religion in America," *Daedalus* (Journal of the American Academy of Arts and Sciences), Winter, 1967. Also R. E. Richey and D. G. Jones, *American Civil Religion* (Harper Forum Books, 1974).

fundamental religious structure of American society, but also
that they have accepted a way of understanding, experiencing
and living their church membership which is determined by
the doctrines and practices of the "American way of life" and
not by the traditional doctrines and practices of their own
Church. It may be argued, as indeed it is, that the legal and
factual "recognition" of Eastern Orthodoxy in America as a
"major faith" has facilitated the decline, if not the total disappearance, of the question often put to the Orthodox that
asks whether they are Protestants or Catholics or even Jews;
and as a result, has given the Orthodox a sense of identity in
American society. While superficially, as in hospital, school,
military and social classification and identification, the Orthodox have certainly gained in self-respect, pride and the general acceptance of their peculiarities—all cardinal virtues of
the American way of life—through legal and factual "recognition," this "victory" has been accompanied by the deeper
weakening (if not the total disappearance) of the Orthodox
Christian vision and way of life among many, if not most, of
the Orthodox themselves.

Adoption of Western Approaches

The adoption of Western approaches to religion is not
new for members of the Orthodox Church. The ways in which
many Orthodox have come to understand and practice their
faith has for centuries been influenced by Roman Catholic and
Protestant modes of thought and piety. This "Western captivity" of the Orthodox has been demonstrated by a number
of scholars.[3] It came about as a result of the rupture in the
living tradition of the Orthodox churches and the absence of
theological and spiritual training of the members of the
Church due to the domination of the Orthodox peoples by
non-Christian powers. In these conditions, thoughtful and
searching members of the Orthodox Church have grown ac-

[3]A. Schmemann, "Russian Theology: 1920-1972, An Introductory Survey,"
and C. Yannaras, "Theology in Present-Day Greece," *Saint Vladimir's Theological Quarterly* 16 (1972).

customed to look to the West for enlightenment and inspiration, and to emulate and imitate their Western brethren in
their approach to religious faith, theological education and
spiritual life. They have accepted Western modes of religious
thought and action, Western questions about man's relationship
with God and with his fellow men, and all too often Western
answers as well. In America this has certainly been the case
for many years, with the roots of this situation existing
already in the Orthodox homelands. While on the one hand
the contact of the Orthodox with the West fostered a sense
(among the Orthodox) of being "different"—more ancient,
venerable, traditional, liturgical—they developed the habit
also of adopting Roman Catholic and Reformed doctrines
and practices where applicable, particularly in polemical situations. For example, it has not been uncommon for the
Orthodox to use Roman Catholic arguments against Protestants, and Protestant arguments against Roman Catholics,
and to form their own religious attitudes and actions on
these bases. In this way, there have appeared not a few members of the Orthodox Church who view their faith as "Roman
Catholicism without the papacy," while others have come to
consider Orthodoxy as a sort of "Protestantism of the Eastern
rite," while still others have been bound in a state of confusion
about what and who they really are.

At present there is little doubt that within American
society the adoption of the American view of religion, and
the American religion itself, by the majority of the Orthodox
is once more a following of the path taken by Roman
Catholics, Protestants and Jews in the life of the nation.
On this point it is interesting to note that when certain members of the Orthodox Church persist in their "traditional
ways," they are considered—often with more understanding
and tolerance by non-Orthodox than by fellow-members of
their own Church—to be "out-of-date" and "underdeveloped."
How often it happens that "progressive" members of the
Orthodox Church present their ideas in terms of "modern-
ization" and "Americanization" with references to the
"others," while the "others" show their kindness to the Orthodox by saying: "We understand. We used to be that way our-

selves. It takes time. . . ." References to religious doctrines and practices in America are virtually never references to what is true or false, to what is right or wrong, to what is meaningful or senseless. They are almost without exception in terms of what is modern or backward, civilized or barbarian, democratic or totalitarian, American or "old country."

In this setting, what has happened, and is still happening, is that the Eastern Orthodox Church in America is taking its place in the nation with Protestants, Catholics and Jews as the "fourth major faith" of Americans. The faith itself is reduced, as are the others, to a matter of "our way" in distinction to "other ways," while all ways are given equal standing in society. And although some ways are still "more equal" than others in certain areas, all are equally expressive of the American way of life, upon which all essentially agree and to which all are essentially devoted.

The "Common Faith"

The content of the "common faith" of Americans, as I see it, is the doctrine that a person may believe and do whatever he or she wishes as long as this belief and action does not conflict with the rights of others to do the same. While this doctrine originated from the need for many Christian denominations to coexist peacefully within the same nation, it developed to include non-Christians as well, primarily Jews, and had the character of being a common faith "under God." There used to be some question about whether Roman Catholics could accept and live within such a system, but history has shown that they can. I believe that today the "under God" character of the "common faith" has been surpassed, with the place of God being assumed by the right of the individual to believe whatever he wishes as long as he accepts the doctrine that it is *this very right itself* which is the supreme dogma of the "common faith." According to this tenet each individual is obliged to follow his way privately, with likeminded, freely-consenting adults, while publicly supporting freedom of conscience for all in "private matters."

Religion—A Private Affair

Religion in general, and belief in God in particular, have come today to be strictly and exclusively "private matters"— the "religion of your choice"—with the result being that members of the various faiths have come to believe that even their participation in their own particular religion is to be understood and practiced on their own terms rather than on those of the specific religious community to which they belong. The various churches and synagogues, in this way, become voluntary societies and corporations which individuals join and belong to in order to practice the "religion of their choice"—in ways which they have decided, with the sole conditions for utilizing the properties, personnel and services of their chosen religious society being the desire to do so and the financial support of the corporate operation. Almost nothing is asked, or is considered proper to be asked, in terms of doctrinal commitment or moral behavior; and when such questions are presented, they are considered a hangover from the less liberated and enlightened past to be tolerated, understood, endured or opposed, depending on how offensive and "un-American" they are. Thus, it is not uncommon for people today not merely to question but openly to reject certain "official teachings" of their particular church bodies and to continue participating in their communal, liturgical and sacramental life —understanding and explaining such participation in their own individual ways. The usage of the term "Christian" in contemporary American language is vivid proof that such an attitude and behavior is present and active with no little force. Witness the following examples:

A person invites his priest to the wedding of his child in a local restaurant. The marriage ceremony is composed by the couple to express their view and style of life. The priest explains that he respects the rights of the couple to act as they wish and that he wishes them well, but that since he is a church pastor, identified with another view of life and marriage which is that

of the churchly community to which at least one of the
couple has previously belonged, he does not consider
it proper to attend the restaurant wedding. The priest
receives the angry reply, "And you're supposed to be
a Christian!"

People come to the priest requesting a church funeral
for a deceased relative. The dead person has not been
in church for decades, has not participated in the
communal and sacramental life of the Church and has
been known to be openly opposed to the moral teachings of the faith. The priest explains that he will do a
burial service if the people want it, but that he cannot
do the normal liturgical service which supposes that
the deceased has been a committed member of the
churchly community. The priest then hears the words,
"And this is supposed to be a Christian church!"

An ecumenical group visits a local Orthodox parish
for the eucharistic liturgy. Some persons express their
desire to receive holy communion. The priest explains
that while he knows that some denominations have
other beliefs and practices, the view of holy communion in the Orthodox Church is that the eucharist
is not only a means for personal sanctification but is
the very expression of the Church herself in which one
participates when he or she is fully committed to the
doctrines, moral teachings and canonical disciplines
of the historical Orthodox community and is totally
identified with it. The priest is then told in no uncer-
tain terms that religion is an individual matter between
the person and God and that the refusal to allow
sacramental participation to anyone who desires it is
"not Christian."

These examples taken from actual experiences may be
considered by some to be rare or extreme, but I am convinced
that they are neither rare nor extreme in the spiritual attitude
which they reveal, nor in the use of the term "Christian"

which is employed to express it. It may well be that most people would be more delicate in their approach, or more "understanding" of the priest as being "behind the times," but as I see it, more and more people are coming to feel as those in the above examples did, and this is definitely a "feeling" more than any clearly thought-out position based on reasoning or rational deduction.

People *feel* extremely uneasy when they are expected to follow communal norms in spiritual and religious matters. Pastors *feel* uneasy when they are obliged to confront people with these expectations. There is the sense that "something is wrong" and that peoples' consciences are being violated. Even the norms of traditional church disciplines are *felt* to be oppressive and binding, demeaning of individual dignity and liberty. They restrict individual rights, are invasions of personal privacy, violations of moral conscience, and reek of old-fashioned dogmatism and bigotry; that is, they are unbecoming for free citizens of modern democratic states in which everyone is equal and free and is obliged to follow his or her own conscience in private affairs.

In contemporary democratic societies individuals must have the freedom to express their religious convictions in ways that they see fit. And churches, which formerly exercised such rights, must now cooperate in seeing that individual freedom reigns supreme by making their services available to all who desire them in the ways that they choose. Not to cooperate in this way is, of course, legally possible in America, but it is not socially and spiritually acceptable. It is considered to be backward and sectarian, closed-minded and undemocratic. Those who wish to act in this way are free to do so under the law, but they are not expected to do so according to the contemporary spirit. If they choose to act in this way, they are excluded from the mainstream of American moral and intellectual life and are tolerated as being strange, if not suspected of being dangerous.

The ironic aspect of this contemporary religious attitude, a point which its proponents would vehemently deny, is that this position itself has become as dogmatic and closed-minded as any specific religious dogmatism has ever been. One simply cannot question or oppose it without being considered anything other than a sectarian crusader out to conquer the infidel and to crush the adversary. This view is held not only by those who would disagree with any religious or moral position presented as objectively true and universally valid, but more sadly, by those who themselves hold such positions. Even churches of the "catholic tradition" have to sell this tradition to their own members, with those doing the "selling" usually labelled as "conservative." The point is that in contemporary America, virtually all people agree that in spiritual matters the choice is between individualistic relativism and crusading sectarianism, and those who accept some religious view as true and right for all people inevitably are forced, voluntarily or involuntarily, to adopt sectarian attitudes and actions. Within such a situation a free and open discussion of spiritual belief and behavior is impossible. There must either be "conversations" and "sharings" in which people describe what they believe and do with no implication that others ought to see things the same way and act accordingly; or else there is high-pressure, hard-sell apologetical evangelism aimed at beating the other in polemical encounter and winning the other to one's side through spiritual conversion. Both ways are utterly American. The first way is accepted by the majority. The second way is tolerated in the minority. To be convinced of this, one need only participate in a typical American religious discussion, whether it be in an inter-faith or ecumenical setting, in an academic or even parochial situation. For Americans today, religion must be either relativistic or sectarian. Any other way is not even understood as possibly existing.

Open Debate and Conflict

There is, I believe, another way. It is the way of traditional Christianity as I see it, a way which should be acceptable to non-Christians as well as Christians. It is the way that I would hope—perhaps, like Abraham, "against hope"—would become the acceptable way for all people, particularly for Americans who have the ideal opportunity to implement it if they so desire. It is the way of free and open debate and even conflict in religious, spiritual and moral matters without prejudices or pressures of any sort, either psychological or social (not to speak of legal or physical), with the purpose of coming to one mind and one heart about the deepest and ultimate issues of human life and destiny. For such a debate to exist there must first of all be the desire to have it exist, with the faith that such a debate could reach some good conclusions if minds are open and hearts are pure, and with the will to reach such conclusions without fear of personal loss or diminution of any sort. People must be ready to expose their personal and corporate religious beliefs and practices to public scrutiny and have them questioned, analyzed and tested as to their value and worth, their power and truth, by persons of different views and experiences. In addition, there must be a genuine love for one another which casts out all self-centeredness and fear, as well as a love for all that is good and true, so that people would be open to see and embrace it wherever, and in whomever, it is to be found. What there cannot be is the attitude that such debate and conflict is hopeless or dangerous, or the attitude that one must defend one's own position at all costs in a closed and self-protective manner out of fear of being put down or swallowed up by others.

Whatever despicable and outrageous attitudes and actions for and against religious belief and practice have existed and still exist, the solution of spiritual conflict and the crown of spiritual development for modern man in democratic societies cannot be a monolithic mainline relativism in all non-scientific, non-technological, non-commercial areas of life, with the toleration of certain sectarians on the fringes— whether they be theistic or atheistic—as evidence of freedom and open-mindedness. This is no solution at all. It is the end of man's spiritual development and moral progress and excludes all chance for human community of any value and depth.

The task of all those who care for the dignity and value of humankind in the modern world and especially in America

—whether or not they are believers in God, but most certainly
if they are—is to defend the principle that men must challenge one another in spirit and in truth so that they might
discover together that which is spiritually and morally genuine
and be united with one another in the fruits of their discovery.
This principle is universally accepted and operative in the
scientific, technological and commercial areas of man's life
in the world today—at least in the free world where some
measure of justice and brotherly concern prevails. It must
become common in the spiritual and moral areas as well. In
the realms of science, technology and commerce, challenge,
debate and conflict are the essential means of development
and progress. People compete and conflict in these areas so
that discovery and achievement become possible and so that
the results of this discovery and achievement may become—
if there be justice and brotherly concern—the common possession of all humankind. There is nothing in these areas which
could be considered as good for some and not for others, as
workable and helpful for some and not for the whole of
humankind. There is no scientific, technological or commercial knowledge, method or skill which is not understood to
be of value and worth to all people given the chance to
possess and use it. The same must be true for the things of the
spirit.

In the realms of morality, spirituality and religion, men
must seek together to discover what is true, good and workable for all. This cannot be done without conflict of ideas,
experiences and methods of spiritual and moral activity and
life. It cannot be done without the conviction that what is
good, true and valuable for one is so for the other and is the
common possession of all. It cannot be done without the
realization that man's spirit, like man's world, is not a "private
affair," and that, as a matter of plain fact, there is no such
thing as a "private matter" in the human community. Humankind is one. It is a body of persons in necessary and essential
interrelation and mutual influence. Human persons are not
isolated individuals cut off from one another in self-enclosed
units of thought and behavior. To act as if this were the case
is to violate reality itself. The knowledge and experience of

one person can be the experience of all, and the most hidden movement within the human spirit is, in fact, an event of universal and cosmic proportions.

Whatever the failures and crimes of Christians in history, the traditional Christian understanding of human being and life is that man's task and destiny lies in a never-ending process of growth and development into an ever-more-perfect inter-personal community, which is at the same time an ever-more-perfect diversity and pluralism of spiritual insight, experience and action. Because of the unqualified freedom necessary for this process to go on, there exists the possibility for deviation and division, a "missing of the mark," a falling away and a falling apart, alienation, estrangement, disunity, decomposition. . . . It is precisely for this reason that mutual challenge and conflict are necessary with mutual questioning and criticism as well as mutual instruction, inspiration and support. While I believe that every person who cares about the quality and destiny of human life must support such a process of spiritual conflict and growth, Christians, of all people, are obliged to foster and defend it. This is the way of Jesus Christ as well as that of his prophets, apostles and martyrs.

Neither Relativist Nor Sectarian

Jesus was not a relativist. Neither was he a sectarian. Whatever one happens to believe about His person and nature, one should see that He was not a "peddler" of some religious doctrine or a "crusader" for some religious sect. He was a man—the man whom many believe to be the incarnation of God—who witnessed to the unity of mankind in freedom, in spirit and in truth. He spoke not about "spiritualities" or "religions" but about goodness, truth, virtue, light and life itself. He was not a "tyrant" of any sort. He exercised no power or force of any kind—political, social, economic, psychological or religious. But he believed that people could know the truth and do good, and so be free and one in human community. When Christians, of all people, resort to individualistic relativism or to crusading sectarianism as the solution to man's spiritual and moral problems and divisions, they immediately cease to be followers of Jesus. If Christians will be followers of Christ, they must freely open themselves to others, not without suffering, conflict and pain, respecting the freedom of others in every area of human life. They must be willing to expose themselves, their views and their actions, to scrutiny and criticism. They must be ready to give reasons and show cause for their beliefs and behavior. They must do this, first of all, before anything else, with one another. And they must do so not merely on academic, bureaucratic or social levels; not through the debates of professional theologians, or the negotiations of organizational officials, or the "sharings" of parlor conversationalists; but in existential, spiritual contact and conflict in order to arrive at one mind, one heart and one body in reality, in attitude and action, in word and in deed, in spirit and in truth. To do this, whether the persons be Christian or not, there must be the desire to be one in fact, and not merely in words or in external actions, or in a "unity" in which certain areas of life are reserved for one's private consumption and enjoyment. All things must be open to all. Nothing must remain hidden. Nothing must remain private. To use the words of the apostle Paul, all men must seek and desire for all people "whatever is true, whatever is honorable, whatever is just, whatever is pure, whatever is lovely, whatever is gracious, if there is any excellence, if there is anything worthy of praise . . ." (Phil. 4:8). And each person must be prepared to recognize and affirm these realities wherever, whenever and in whomever they exist, and to call for judgment when he considers them violated or destroyed.

There is no question but that people disagree and will continue to disagree about what in reality is true, honorable, just, pure, lovely, gracious, excellent and worthy of praise. They will disagree about where and in whom such spiritual qualities are present and active. For this very reason there must be dialogue and debate, contact and conflict, demonstration and testing. The point here is not about the *content* of these realities; the point is rather about the necessary *method* of their discovery for the benefit of human unity, progress and development. The method simply cannot be that of relativistic individualism or polemical sectarianism if there is to be any hope at all for spiritual growth and achievement among people.

As we Americans enter our third century of national existence, it is my hope that an "American way" will develop in which man's "life, liberty and pursuit of happiness" will be adequate to the true dignity of the human spirit. My hope, also, is that specifically the Christian life in this new way will be neither the peacefully-coexisting conglomeration of relativistic individual and corporate opinions, nor the crusading confrontations of self-righteous and closed-minded sectarians, but the free and gracious life of spiritual communion and conflict revealed to the world in Christ who offers "all the fulness of God" to those who seek Him.

7

Witness and Service in Orthodox Christian Life

At a recent ecumenical gathering a colleague of mine was asked what he thought was the task of the Orthodox Church in the modern world. Without taking thought he replied, "To preserve people's sanity." Being somewhat surprised and embarrassed by his spontaneous response, my friend had then to try to explain what he meant by his remark. This paper about witness and service in Orthodox Christian life is also an explanation and a certain elaboration of the strange response of my friend. I too believe that we modern people, certainly we in America, live in a world—even an *ecclesiastical* world—which has in a deep and serious way become "insane." And I too believe that the sole haven of "sanity" is the Orthodox Christian Church.

"Insanity" in my present definition of the term has two meanings. First, I use the term to mean a lack of wholeness and integrity; a falling-apart of human being and life; a disintegration and decomposition of man's world; a loss of cohesion and meaning to the totality of man's experiences, visions and actions. And secondly, I use the term "insanity" simply as "madness"—perhaps a quiet, unspectacular, everyday madness, but madness all the same; a triumph of irrationality and foolishness; a breakdown of logic and consistency in human thought and behavior; an allegiance to forms, sometimes a passionate and violent allegiance, with a denial of their content, meaning and power, a denial sometimes equally passionate and equally violent. In a word, I use the term "insanity" to mean the loss of touch with reality—the reality of oneself, one's neighbors, human history, the world, the Church, God Himself.

Forms of Insanity

The causes of the present "insanity" as well as its forms are many and varied. One might even say they are "legion." But all of them, it seems to me, appear to be rooted in one factor which is pervasive in our time. This is the propensity of people today to deal with the complications, complexities and confusions of life by reducing man to one or another of his human elements or expressions, and then to attempt to understand and explain everything about man and his world in terms of this one aspect of his existence. Thus, for example, for some people man is simply a body, a biologically determined animal with feelings, emotions and drives, and everything is understood and explained in this particular perspective. Others reduce man to a sexual being, and root everything in human being and behavior, culture and history, to man's sexual component. Others deny man's bodily being, and attempt to transform man into an "angel," a spirit struggling to be free of his imprisonment in time, in history, in his material condition. Still others see the fundamental and determining aspect of man to be exactly his temporality, his being rooted in history, his being formed and explained by the temporal process. Others refer to economic and political factors as basic and determining, while others refer to "religion" and the "mystical experience." Still others identify man as essentially an "individual," and stress each person's uniqueness and independence from others, his need to discover his own separate and incomparable "identity," while others see man as fundamentally a "social being," striving for relationships with others which are "meaningful, creative and fulfilling." Others still, overwhelmed by the tragedy of man's being in the world, his suffering and death, find everything to be absurd, and embrace "absurdity" itself as man's basic and final reality. And others yet, in an effort to suppress the perplexing and painful realities of life in an evil and death-bound world, attempt to "accentuate the positive" by blinding themselves to everything "negative" through the "pursuit of happiness" in the carnal and spiritual pleasures and activities of their particular choosing. Thus, the bedroom or the sports arena, the concert hall or the library, the restaurant or the meditation center, the political party or the ethnic-culture movement becomes the center of life and the source and locus of its meaning and purpose. But whatever the simplification, whatever the reduction, the result is the same. It is "insanity," because it is in every case a suppression of something essential and integral to human being and life. It is "insanity" because it is, in theological terms, a loss of man's "catholic consciousness" and a destruction of his "catholic being" as a creature made in the image and likeness of God in whom everything is held together in harmony, cohesion and perfect integration.

It is for this reason that Christians claim Christ to be the only solution against "insanity," for in Him alone do *all* things hold together, and in Him alone does *every* aspect and element of man's being and life find its meaning and purpose. In a word, in Him alone does man become and remain *whole.*

Reductions of Christ

At this point, however, we are obliged to confront another difficulty peculiar to our time. This is the fact that Christ Himself is all too often co-opted into one or another of the many simplifications and reductions of man that are produced by the "insane" of the world. Christians themselves have fallen victim to "insanity." The clear demonstration of this, at least to my mind, is revealed in the many different and contradictory "christs" which are available today for man's choosing. There is the christ of secular humanism and the christ of religious mysticism, the christ of political activ-ism and the christ of cultic ritualism. There is the christ of the feminists and the christ of the nationalists, the christ of the poor and the oppressed and the christ of the powerful and the possessing. There is the christ of the Marxist critique of history and the christ of the psychotherapeutic analyses of human behavior. There is the "hidden" christ of the non-Christian religions, and the "revealed" christ of the fundamentalist preachers. There is the christ of the process thinkers and the christ of the existentialist—or essentialist—philosophers. There is the "sweet" christ of the pietists and the "avenging" christ of the freedom-fighters. In my own churchly circles there is even the christ who is called upon as a necessary element in the resurrection and reestablishment of the Russian, Ukrainian or Albanian nations. And in my secular social setting there is the christ who is considered necessary for the maintenance of the benign and tolerant comforts of middle- and upper-class America, the christ of the "American way of life" whose main task is to guarantee the security and well-being of the American nation for its divinely-mandated mission of being the leader in the world in all that is bigger and better, more prosperous and comfortable, more affluent and efficient.

The Holy Scriptures say that there have always been for people "many gods and many lords." What we see in our time is also "many christs." And we hear the "insane" among Christians crying out: "Lo, He is here! Lo, He is there!" And we ask, with many others who hear the discordant cries: Where is the real Christ? Who is He? How is He? What is He? Is He at all? Or is He not, after all, whatever and whoever anyone thinks or wishes Him to be?

We Orthodox Christians answer, of course, that Christ is. But can we see and know Him as He really is? Can we reveal Him to others? Can we bear witness to Him and serve Him? Can we serve others by serving and bearing witness to Him? In a word, is there the possibility for "sanity," if indeed, as we claim, the salvation from "insanity" is to be found in Christ and only in Him? We are back to my friend and his claim: the mission of the Orthodox Church in the modern world is "to preserve people's sanity." The Church, we believe, is the haven of salvation from "insanity," including the "insanity" of Christians who have—as it were with the Bible in one hand and some philosophical, political, psychotherapeutic or religious ideology in the other—produced in our time a pleroma of christs to go with the pleroma of gods and world-views born of the reduction of man to one or another of his human elements or expressions.

The Church As the Whole Christ

The *Church* is the key. This is our message today about witness and service in Christian life, and about Christian witness and service in the contemporary world. The Church is the key because it is only in the Church that Christ is to be known as He really is in the fulness of His divine and human being and life. It is only in the Church that the "sane" Christ can be met, loved, witnessed and served in the wholeness and integrity of His theandric reality; and through Him, the "sane" God and the "sane" man. The "sane" Christ is the Christ of the Church, we say. And indeed, we dare to say it, the "sane" Christ is in a real sense Christ *and* the Church: the whole Christ, head and body—*totus Christus, caput et corpus.*

The fundamental *mission* of Orthodox Christians today is to serve man and the world by bearing witness to the fact that there is the Christ who saves, and that this Christ is present now in the midst of the earth in His Church. And this Christ alone is the source of man's being, the purpose of man's history, the end of man's desires, the very *Life* of man's life. Man is made for God. He is made to "be god" by the grace and good pleasure of his Maker in whose image and likeness he is formed, male and female. Human being and life is senseless without God. There is no explanation of man without God, no understanding of man without God and no life for man without God . . . and we say *God* and not *religion*. But people do not know this. Even many Christians do not know this, not in its real meaning and power. It is not their immediate experience, although it is, we would say, the secret source of their striving and the hidden cause of their disquiet and lack of inner satisfaction and peace.

Man Without God

People do not know that they are made for God because they suppress the fact, or the fact is suppressed in them by the wickedness of their fellow men—their parents, their teachers, their national and political leaders and even, not seldomly, their pastors and priests. People are often victims—although, once again, not seldomly all-too-willing victims indeed. People must be told that the source and the goal of their being and life is God. They must be reminded and informed of their true nature and calling. They must be convinced that the root cause of their sorrows and fears, their dissatisfactions and frustrations, is the *"ungodliness and wickedness of men* who by their wickedness suppress the truth" (Rom. 1:18). For there is indeed a suppression of the truth due to wickedness and sin. The prophets of the Lord describe it with explosive and agonizing lucidity. And the apostles, especially Paul, are no less pathetic and powerful:

> For what can be known of God is plain to them, because God has shown it to them. Ever since the creation of the world His invisible nature, namely, His power and divinity, has been clearly perceived in the things that have been made. So they are without excuse; for although they knew God, they did not honor Him as God or give thanks to Him, but they became futile in their thinking and their senseless minds were darkened. . . . Therefore God gave them up in the lusts of their hearts to impurity . . . because they exchanged the truth about God for a lie and worshipped and served the creature rather than the Creator. . . . And since they did not see fit to acknowledge God, God gave them up to a base mind and to improper conduct. They were filled with all manner of evil, covetousness, malice. Full of envy, murder, strife, deceit, malignity,

they are gossips, slanderers, haters of God, insolent, haughty, boastful, inventors of evil, disobedient to parents, foolish, faithless, heartless, ruthless . . . (Rom. 1:18-32).

Hear the word of the Lord, O people of Israel, for the Lord has a controversy with the inhabitants of the land. There is no faithfulness or kindness, and no knowledge of God in the land; there is swearing, lying, killing, stealing and committing adultery; they break all bounds and murder follows murder. Therefore the land mourns, and all who dwell in it languish, and also the beasts of the field and the birds of the air, and even the fish of the sea are taken away. . . . for with you is my contention, O priest. You shall stumble by day, the prophet also shall stumble with you by night; and I will destroy your mother. My people are destroyed for lack of knowledge; because you have rejected knowledge, I reject you from being a priest to me. And since you have forgotten the law of your God, I also will forget your children. The more they increased, the more they sinned against me; I will change their glory into shame. They feed on the sin of my people; they are greedy for their iniquity. And it shall be like people, like priest; I will punish them for their ways, and requite them for their deeds. They shall eat and not be satisfied; they shall play the harlot, but not multiply; because they have forsaken the Lord. . . . (Hosea 4:1-10; see also, *e.g.,* Jeremiah 23, Ezekiel 34, Isaiah 5, *etc.*).

This is the condition of *man without God,* the condition of people opposed to God. The witness of Christians and their service to the world is to testify to this reality. And their witness and service is to proclaim and to prove that Jesus Christ comes into the world and enters people's lives to turn this all around. He comes to restore the fallen condition of man. He comes to reverse the course of his corrupted destiny. He comes to recreate his world. He comes, in a word, to put everything back together again and to direct everything once more upon its proper course. He comes, so that in Him the true God might make "known to us in all wisdom and insight the mystery of His will" which is "to unite all things in Him, things in heaven and things on earth" (Eph. 1:9-10). He comes so that in and through Him all things might be renewed by being "filled with all the fulness of God" (Eph. 3:19).

The Christ We Witness

The Christ who comes and enters our life, we bear witness, is not a "mere man." He is the eternal Word of God, the one by and for whom all things are made. He is the uncreated Image of God according to which all people and things are fashioned and formed. He is the only-begotten Son of the ever-existing Father who is above all and through all and in us all, through Him. He is the first-born of all creation who is before all things, the one in whom all things hold together. He is the head of His body, the Church. He is the beginning, the first-born of the dead that He might be truly the first in *all* things. He is the one in whom the fulness of divinity dwells bodily, the one in whom all people can come to fulness of life. He is the divine Son of Man, the Heavenly Man, the last and final Adam. He is the one who makes God known. He is the person whose *mind* every person must have if he will be sane, human and godlike:

Have this mind in you, which you have in Christ Jesus, who, though He was in the form of God, did not count equality with God a thing to be grasped, but emptied Himself, taking the form of a slave, being born in the likeness of men. And being found in human form He humbled Himself and became obedient unto death, even death on a cross. Therefore God has highly exalted Him and bestowed upon Him the name which is above every name, that at the name of Jesus every knee should bow, in heaven and on earth, and

under the earth, and every tongue confess that Jesus
Christ is Lord, to the glory of God the Father (Phil.
2:5-11).

Christ is, in His coming to the world, the *Godman*. He is one
of the Holy Trinity; the divine person who has become
human; the human being whom the divine person—the uncreated Logos, Son and Image of God—has become, for us
men, and for our salvation. This is the essence of the Christian
message and world-view, the essential truth to which all
witness must be borne and all service rendered.

And the Word became flesh and dwelt among us, full
of grace and truth; we have beheld His glory, glory as
of the only-begotten Son from the Father . . . and
from His fulness have we all received, grace upon
grace . . . no man has seen God at any time; the only-
begotten Son who is in the bosom of the Father, He
has made Him known (John 1:14-18).

Christians know this and bear witness to it because they
experience it in the Church. They experience Him, here and
now, in the life of His Church, just as He is, in all the fulness
of His divine humanity. Christ is with us now: this is the
Christian witness. God is with us in Him. Others may have
seen and heard and touched Him as He was in the days of
His flesh, but we know Him as He is now in the fulness of
His glory. The "days of His flesh" are over and gone. We
have no need to strive to revive, retrieve or relive them,
certainly not by scholarly, psychological or meditative means.
Jesus Christ is no longer as He was in His days on earth in
the form of a slave. He is present now in His people with God
His Father by the power of God's Spirit in "the Church which
is His body, the fulness of Him who fills all in all" (Eph.
1:23).

From now on we regard no one from a human point
of view (*kata sarka*, "according to the flesh"); even
though we once regarded Christ from a human point

of view, we regard Him thus no longer. Therefore, if any one is in Christ, he is a new creation; the old has passed away, behold, the new has come (2 Cor. 5:16-17).

The old has passed away; the new has come. The "new" is the Church, the final and everlasting covenant of God with man, the Kingdom of God on earth. The Church in her mystical reality is the foretaste and experience now of the new age to come, the new life of the new creature in the new heaven and the new earth. For the Lord said, "Behold, I make all things new!" And He has done so through the crucifixion and resurrection of Christ who is God incarnate. The knowledge and experience of this saving fact is given to man in the life of Christ's Church. Indeed the Church herself, in her very substance and being, *is* this experience. *Extra ecclesiam nulla salus.* Outside the Church there is no salvation because, as we believe and have come to know, *salvation is the Church.*

Christians, certainly we Orthodox Christians, *have nothing to offer people and the world but Christ and the Church.* And it is our conviction that there is nothing else to be offered and nothing else that is necessary. Our witness is to this conviction; our service, to this end. In our time, however, there are specific human needs and desires which cry out for fulfillment, specific cries which arise in the hearts of men which reach our ears, clamoring for concern and attention. If we say that Christ and the Church are the answer to these crying needs, we must be aware of what they are and be prepared to demonstrate *how* their ultimate satisfaction can be attained only in Christ and the Church. And we must be ready to make every effort and sacrifice to verify our claims by our actions, witnessing and serving with a love "not in words and speech, but in deed and in truth" (1 John 3:18). Let us now attempt, at least by way of example, to address ourselves to some of the specific needs and desires of people which are expressed very strongly in our day.

Justice

First there is the issue of social, political and economic *justice*. Human beings want justice and have every right to demand it to the greatest possible measure that it can be attained on this earth. Christians must bear witness to this fact and must serve the cause of justice in human life in all of its forms. There is a great measure of injustice in the world: oppression, exploitation, inequality, tyranny. Some people have possessions and power and others are deprived and victimized. Some people are free to determine their destiny on the earth, at least in certain external and social ways, while others are locked into their lot in life without the power of controling, choosing or changing their ways of living and working. The Christian teaching is that injustice in all of its forms is rooted in wickedness and sin. It is not the result of some accident of history or biology. Where there is *injustice*, there is necessarily *guilt*. Where there is injustice, someone, somewhere, is somehow responsible. Injustice does not simply happen. It is caused by the evils of men. The Christ of the Church, who is Himself the fulfillment of the law and the prophets with their unyielding demands for justice among men, promised to establish justice in His Kingdom at the end of the ages. This is an essential part of His service as the Messiah of God. He Himself predicts that, until He comes again in glory, there will be no perfect justice on the earth. But He Himself also demands that people, certainly *His* people, hunger and thirst for justice and do all in their power to see that it triumphs in human life, here and now. And He judges the acts of men by this rule: all men, both those who explicitly know Him and those who do not.

> For He will render to every man according to his works; to those who by patience in well-doing seek for glory and honor and immortality, He will give eternal life, but for those who are factious and do not obey the truth, but obey wickedness, there will be wrath and fury. There will be tribulation and distress for

every human being who does evil, the Jew first and
also the Greek, but glory and honor and peace for
every one who does good, the Jew first and also the
Greek. For God shows no partiality (Rom. 2:6-10).

In the struggle for justice the Lord sides with the victimized and the oppressed. He condemns the tyrannous. He
throws down the mighty. He exalts the lowly. He judges the
rich who set their hearts on their wealth and multiply their
possessions at the expense of the exploited. The fact that
the poor will always be with us, as Jesus said, does *not* allow
human beings to be callous and indifferent to the needs of
their fellow creatures. The fact that perfect justice will be
established in the Kingdom to come does not free human
beings from establishing justice now, to the measure possible.
On the contrary, it compels them to do so.

But if any one has the world's goods and sees his
brother in need, yet closes his heart against him, how
does God's love abide in him? Little children, let us
not love in word or in speech but in deed and in truth
(1 John 3:17-18).

If a brother or sister is ill-clad and in lack of daily food,
and one of you says to them, "Go in peace, be warmed
and filled," without giving them the things needed for
the body, what does it profit? (James 2:14-17).

Come now, you rich, weep and howl for the miseries
that are coming upon you. . . . Behold the wages of
the laborers who mowed your fields, which you kept
back by fraud, cry out; and the cries of the harvesters
have reached the ears of the Lord of hosts. You have
lived on the earth in luxury and in pleasure; you have
fattened your hearts in a day of slaughter. You have
condemned, you have killed the righteous man; he
does not resist you (James 5:1-6).

These words of Christ's apostles are no less violent and uncompromising than the words of His Old Testament prophets. The Lord sides with the oppressed and favors the poor. *He Himself became poor,* being the owner of everything, so that by His poverty we all might become rich and inherit everything in the Kingdom of God (cf. 2 Cor. 8:9). And in this world He rewards justice in ways known to Himself, according to His inscrutable and unfathomable providence which is always beneficent. While favoring and blessing the poor and the oppressed, however, the Lord does not necessarily join their political party, or accept their economic ideology, or endorse their philosophical world-view. And He certainly judges their sins, as He does those of the rich, being Himself the perfect practitioner of justice. "The rich and poor meet together, the Lord is the maker of them all" (Prov. 22:2). God in Christ is with the oppressed and victimized in their sorrow and affliction; but He is not necessarily with them in their attitudes and actions.

Christ is not a socialist or a capitalist, a monarchist or a democrat, a communist or a fascist. He accepts no other vision of human life than His own. He does not condescend to error, or commiserate with stupidity, or make accommodation with lies, wherever they are found. And human beings are called to accept His vision and nobody else's. This is their only recourse to "sanity" and their only salvation from the snares of the deceivers, on the right hand and on the left, including the deceivers who cover their deceit with His name.

Christ is king and subject, master and slave, ruler and servant. He is known and worshipped this way in the life of His Church. He cannot be co-opted into any earthly program and action which denies any aspect of His theandric being and life as Lord of the universe and its crucified victim. In serving the cause of justice in the world, Christians must themselves be just in every way, whatever their social and economic status, political persuasion or ideological position in any given instance and situation. They must remain free to condemn every injustice, wherever it is found, including even their churchly institutions. And in this their service, they must bear witness to the fact that no earthly party is without sin, and that no human society will ever be trans-

formed by human means alone into the Kingdom of God.
This does not mean that Christians are to remain aloof and
uncommitted in political and social movements and actions.
It does mean, however, that they are to remain inwardly free
and detached, preserved from the "insanity" of selling their
souls to an earthly cause and depersonalizing themselves into
mindless members of a collective crusade in which they are
compelled to sell their divine birthright of spiritual freedom
for a mess of secular, material pottage.

We members of the Orthodox Church stand judged on the
issue of human justice in this world with all people. In a
sense we are even more guilty for our sins in this regard than
others because we claim to be God's people and children of
God's Kingdom. For, as Jesus has said, "everyone to whom
much is given, of him will much be required" (Luke 12:48);
and we dare to pray in our liturgy: "Grant us Your peace
and Your love, O Lord our God, for You have given all
things unto us" (St. Basil's Liturgy).

If we have indeed been given not simply *much*, but *all
things* from the Lord, then we, of all people, must be lovers
and servants of justice on the earth. We must repent not only
for our personal sins, but for our acceptance of secular ideologies in place of the Gospel of Christ, often covering these
ideologies of men with the name of God. We must repent
of our uncritical approbation of secular programs, often with
ecclesiastical approval, as the supposed means to a just society, which society is, in fact, the one most beneficial not to
the greatest number of people, but merely to ourselves. We
have been guilty, in fact, of witnessing and serving not Christ
and the Church, but something other and something else of
our own making.

Perfect justice lies only in Christ and the Church; and
the most just society on this earth, whatever its form at
the moment—which is always relatively determined in any
time and place by the pragmatic considerations which the
given situation demands—, must be inspired and patterned
after the Kingdom of God. If we will witness this truth
and serve its realization among men, we must accept it
ourselves and express it in our behavior and actions as

persons, societies and ecclesiastical bodies. We Orthodox have a long way to go in this regard. The events of our recent history show this. We have failed in many ways, for example in the failure of church leaders in imperial Russia to establish and defend the independence and integrity of the Church from state interference and control; in the failure of many clergymen to be received by their people as fellow-sufferers and servants in the Lord, rather than as masters and overlords; in the injustice and cruelty which Orthodox Christians inflicted on each other in the Balkans because of ethnic and national differences; in the divisions and animosities which developed between Orthodox Christians in America because of the national and political disagreements primarily of church leaders, for which the people continue to pay the price; in the alliances in so many countries between church leaders and one or another political party which has caused the disintegration and demoralization of churchly life and has made the Church an object of derision and disgust in the eyes of the people who are abandoned to their own devices in finding direction and purpose to their existence on earth. We must be humble and courageous enough to acknowledge our faults and to allow ourselves to be judged by the doctrine and worship of our own Church which is witnessed in her scriptures, her sacraments and her saints.

Freedom

In relation to the issue of justice, we have made reference to the fact that people today also cry out for *freedom*. People want to be free in many different ways. In addition to the movements for political, economic, social and religious freedom, there are also many other kinds of liberation movements, particularly in the West. We have in America everything from the "Gay Liberation Movement" of the homosexuals to the "Gray Liberation Movement" of the elderly, with perhaps the most widespread and popular movement being that for the "liberation of women."

Once again we turn to Christ and the Church in order to discover what true freedom is and what genuine liberation is all about. When people cry for freedom from injustice, and the injustice is real, then there can be no doubt where Christians and all human beings must be in the struggle. But we must bear witness in Christ that what often passes for a movement of legitimate liberation is in fact a striving, in knowledge or in ignorance, for greater enslavement and more treacherous bondage. In these cases, human beings must be set free from the "insanity" of their desires by the experience of God and the truth which is from God, which is, in itself, the most fundamental guarantee of genuine liberty.

> Jesus then said to the Jews who believed in Him, "If you continue in My word, you are truly My disciples, and you will know the truth and the truth will make you free . . . everyone who commits sin is a slave to sin. The slave does not continue in the house forever; the son continues forever. So if the Son makes you free, you will be free indeed" (John 8:31-36).

True freedom in the Christian perspective consists neither in passive resignation to one's earthly fate nor in active rebellion against the conditions and structures of life in which one finds oneself in the world. It consists rather in the joyful acceptance of one's earthly conditions provided by a gracious, wise and loving God who has given each person his being and life as the best possible circumstances for fulfilling one's earthly vocation in the service of God and man. Belief in divine providence and in the fact that each person has a unique vocation from God, in the place where he is called, to sanctify, transfigure and redeem the specific conditions of his life in ways provided and revealed by God, is fundamental to the Christian view of human liberation.

Man is truly free when he *loves* his life in the world, his time, his place, his calling and his task; when he believes that his life is the best one for him in which to fulfill his vocation; when he *struggles* to work out his salvation in obedience to God and service to his fellows within the situation in which God has put him; and when he trusts that God's will will be done in his life—the will of God whose ways and thoughts are not ours—if only he will be obedient to God's commandments in every smallest and seemingly most insignificant detail of his daily activity. Such a person is truly free because, paradoxically, he both accepts his human situation and condition and, at the same time, is not determined or bound by it. Jesus Himself is the most perfect example of such behavior. He embraced the conditions of His earthly life, was subject to "every human institution" (to use the apostle's expression) for God's sake: to His family, society, nation, religion, political situation. And yet He resisted every temptation and rejected every evil which the same "human institutions" offered Him in the effort to divert Him from His messianic vocation to save the world. In this way Jesus was truly free; indeed He was the only truly free man who ever lived, and by His freedom He achieved the liberation of all people and the whole of creation.

It is to *this* freedom of Christ that all human beings are called. It is the freedom of the "glorious liberty of the children of God" (Rom. 8:21) guaranteed and realized in human persons by the indwelling of the Spirit of God. It is the freedom not to miss the mark of one's human vocation by making life in this world an end in itself; or by defining one's entire being and life by life in this world; or by yielding to the wickedness and evil which a self-centered, this-worldly life necessarily demands.

> For you were called to freedom, brethren; only do not use your freedom as an opportunity for the flesh, but through love be servants one of another. For the whole law is fulfilled in one word, "You shall love your neighbor as yourself." But if you bite and devour one another take heed that you are not consumed by one another (Gal. 5:13-14).

180 ALL THE FULNESS OF GOD

The only genuine freedom for man is the freedom *not to sin;* it is certainly not the freedom not to be sinned against! Man is set free in Christ because he is enabled by the grace of the Holy Spirit to fulfill the law of God in his life in perfect freedom and self-control. For, the apostle says, he who looks to God's "perfect law, the law of liberty" sees not only any more his own "natural face," but the face of Christ, which is indeed his true face; and when he perseveres in his actions to be obedient to God's law in every way, being utterly faithful in little, then he is "set over much" and receives the blessing of true freedom from God (cf. James 1:22-26; Matt. 25).

Only in Christ and the Church do we find the image and meaning of true freedom which is the liberation from the "law of sin and death" which works in our earthly members: "For the law of the Spirit and life in Christ Jesus has set me free from the law of sin and death" (Rom. 8:2). Only in Christ and the Church do we find the pattern for the right relationships of human beings to each other, to themselves, to their bodies, to their sexuality, to their psychic and emotional experiences, to their earthly institutions and histories, to their death . . . and to God Himself. This "right relationship" is true liberty. When a person finds it and lives it he is free indeed. Without it there is only enslavement to "empty deceit, according to human tradition, according to the elemental spirits of the universe" (Col. 2:8), and bondage to the graceless powers of "this age" whose "form is passing away" (1 Cor. 7:31).

True freedom is in Christ and the Church as God's Kingdom on earth. Our witness and service in the world is to have people see this and know this, and so to be freed from the futility of their delusions and rebellions, as well as from the frustrations, dissatisfactions and disappointments which inevitably result when their earthly needs and desires, even when satisfied, still prove insufficient and unfulfilling.

Identity and Community

The discussion of freedom organically leads to another of the great issues of our time: man's quest for *identity* and *community*. In a complex and rapidly changing world people lose the sense of who they are and why they exist. In order to find themselves and others, they often reduce themselves to one or another of their earthly aspects or expressions, as we mentioned above. Not the least of the possible reductions of human life is that provided by *ethnic and national determinations* and/or *religious and ideological affiliations*, with the two often combined into one. If people have become "secularized" and have lost personal identification with any particular history or culture (as often happens in America, especially with the young), they may seek their identity through "mysticism" or "religious experiences," or through an internal search into the depths of their psyches, using psychotherapeutic analysis as the way to the discovery of their "true self." Not seldomly the problem of individual identity is connected with a person's sexuality, with the desire for personal or professional success or achievement, or with pathological complexes of one sort or another. Once again it is the Christian witness and an essential aspect of Christian service to demonstrate that one finds oneself ultimately—one's true and whole self, the self infinitely loved by God—only in Christ and the Church.

Christ is, in a sense, each person's "true self." He is the uncreated Image of God according to which each created image is made. He is the only-begotten Son of God, the eternal Child of God, in whom all of God's children find their proper relationship with their Fatherly Source, and so with each other as well. Each human being is a "word spoken by God." And Christ is God's divine and perfect Word in whom all creaturely words are rooted and grounded, finding their meaning and purpose, their being and their life.

In the experience of the Church, the encounter with Christ is also an encounter with one's true self in its wholeness, and with the real selves of others, with the possibility of discovering who one really is and why one really exists and what one really ought to be and to do in this world. In order for this encounter to take place, all other forms of self-identification and self-realization must be forsaken. This is the Gospel teaching. "If any one comes to me and does not hate his own father and mother and wife and children and brothers and sisters, yes, even his very own life (*psyche*), he cannot be My disciple . . . so therefore whoever does not renounce all that he has cannot be My disciple" . . . and cannot, thereby, discover his true self or realize his true being and calling (cf. Luke 14:25-33). This is the radical teaching of Jesus:

> If any man would come after me, let him deny himself and take up his cross and follow Me. For whoever would save his life (*psyche*) will lose it; and whoever loses his life for My sake and the gospel's will save it. For what does it profit a man to gain the whole world and forfeit his life? For what can man give in return for his life?

Man cannot find himself in himself. This is the Christian teaching. He can only find himself in self-denying, self-emptying love for the other: the Other who is God, and all others who are God's creaturely children, images and words. The way of discovering one's identity and of finding oneself and others cannot be by meditation or introspection or analysis of one's thoughts and behavior. Still less can it be by identifying oneself with a race, nation, party, sex, class or religion. It can only be by abandoning all those things, even one's religion, as ends in themselves; and forsaking one's own soul and life in this world for the sake of God and His Kingdom, which is for the sake of Christ and His gospel, which is for the sake of loving and serving all human beings and all of God's creatures in spirit and in truth. This alone is the way to self-discovery and self-realization. And this alone is also the way to the discovery of genuine community with others.

True *community*, which so many people long for today with overwhelming desire, is achieved only by the abandonment of self in love for the other. This is the secret so powerfully revealed by Jesus, the secret which all of the great mystical saints discovered in their union with God. Man discovers himself and others by forsaking himself and by living for others, with others, and even "in" others, with compassionate, co-suffering love. When the self-forgetfulness and self-abandonment of a person is perfect, or to the measure that it is perfect, the lover no longer is concerned about his *relationships* with the other; he is interested only in the *other himself*. God is this way. The Father Almightly is not an isolated, self-enclosed and self-contained being. He is not the "great individual in the sky." He is not the Alone, alone with Himself in self-contemplating satisfaction and bliss. He is rather a *person*, a perfect, divine person who realizes His divine perfection by naturally expressing and realizing Himself in the person of another to whom He communicates His perfect divine being in love. In a word, God is essentially a *Father* and has with Himself, as an element of His own perfect personhood and being, His only-begotten Son in and with whom, so to speak, He discovers His own "true self" as the God who is Love (cf. 1 John 4:7). The only-begotten Son of God, incarnate in this world as Jesus, is the "son of God's love," as St. Paul puts it, the "icon of the invisible God," the "radiance of His glory and the express image of His person (*hypostasis*)" (Col. 1:14-15, Heb. 1:3). God the Father's very perfection consists in His self-sharing love. He shares His divinity with others and through them expresses and realizes His own divine perfection. He does this "in a divine manner" with His Son and His Spirit, and "by grace" with His creatures who are the created manifestations of His divine perfection and glory, reflecting His Word and His Spirit in their creaturely realization of His divine being and life.

Human beings, like the God in whose image they are made, are essentially and necessarily *persons-in-community*. They are not individuals seeking relationships. Neither are they a collective mass, seeking individuality. They are persons in essential communal relationships by their very nature as reflections of God, the Blessed Trinity, the metaphysical archetype of their being and life. The tendency today either to isolate man in his individuality or to submerge him into an impersonal collective and then to try to forge out for him some sort of "meaningful relationships" is doomed to failure. It is doomed to failure because it is an ontological impossibility to treat man in this way. Human beings are simply not like this and cannot be approached and treated in this fashion. Once again, it is only Christ and the Church that can save people from this "insanity."

In Christ and the Church the absolute uniqueness of the human person is guaranteed and perfected through communal existence with others, in which the human being becomes more and more "himself" as he becomes more and more an incomparable and eternally valuable member of the community which is the body of Christ (cf. 1 Cor. 12). As the body of Christ in her mystical reality, the Church is the gracious realization among human persons of the tri-personal nature of God. In the Church in which all are "members one of another" in truth and in love, being of one mind and heart and having one soul, each member grows up to maturity in Christ by the sovereign freedom of the Spirit of God (cf. Acts 4:32, Eph. 4). Only in the Church does a human being find himself in community with others, enhancing and developing his personal uniqueness without being absorbed into a soulless collective in which he loses his personal identity.

The Church Is the Key

The Church is the key. We have said this already, and we must say it again. Our reference is to the Church as the *whole Christ, head and body,* the Church as the sacramental and mystical reality of the Kingdom of God in the midst of the earth, a reality which is objectively present, incarnate in history with a concrete content and form guaranteed to its being in all places and times by the Spirit of

God. This is the Church which is officially constituted in the liturgical assembly, centered in the eucharist, in which the living Father is known and adored through Jesus Christ, His Son and Word, by the indwelling of His Holy Spirit. This is the Church which reveals itself as the Kingdom of God and the recreation of the world in sacramental celebration, the Church whose form and content is thoroughly biblical, defined and shaped by the scriptures of Israel and the apostolic community who saw the risen Jesus and confessed Him as Messiah and Lord. This is the Church which the prophets foretold, the apostles preached, the martyrs witnessed and the saints preserved . . . and continue to preserve. It is the Church of the fathers and councils, the Church of the holy tradition and the apostolic succession which claims an unbroken continuity, identity, solidarity and integrity through the ages as the one, holy, catholic and apostolic Church of Christ, the "pillar and the bulwark of the truth" (2 Tim. 3:15). This is the Church whose genuine participants—the persons who communicate in the body not unto judgment or condemnation but for forgiveness and healing and life everlasting—are always revealed as true witnesses and servants by their self-emptying suffering in love for the truth and the good of the brethren. This is the real Church, the Church in which we confess our faith when we recite the Nicene Creed, which we do daily since the day when we became her unworthy members by baptism, chrismation and holy communion.

The Church will exist until the end of the ages. This is the promise of Christ. It cannot be destroyed by the will of men or the powers of darkness. But it can be betrayed and denied by the sinners who are in it. It can be participated for condemnation and judgment. It can be disobeyed and unheeded by the very persons who are responsible for its mission and life in this world, its very own members who are judged by its truth. And here, once again, we Orthodox Christians are in need of repentance.

Our churchly life at present is in lamentable condition. Our ecclesiastical institutions and structures are in deplorable shape. We do not practice what we ourselves preach, not

merely in our personal lives, but in our ecclesiastical dealings. When we talk theology, we agree. When we defend
the Holy Trinity and the Godmanhood of Christ, we are
one. When we describe the mystical being of the Church,
we concur. When we celebrate the mysteries of salvation,
we sing with one voice. When we offer our prayers, we
speak with one mouth. *But when we act, we are separated
and divided.* When we move into the area of practical application, of living witness and service, we part company.
Not only do our legitimate and acceptable political and cultural differences keep us apart—that is understandable and
of little crucial importance. What is much worse and wholly
unjustified is that we allow the "insanity" of the world to
possess us. We become irrational and foolish. We become
inconsistent and discordant with our own theoretical doctrines. We deny our own theology and worship. We betray
our own vision.

Our patriarchal ecclesiastical structure, glorified for its
venerable antiquity, is for the most part, *nominal and
pretentious.* It applies in real life to almost nothing that is
real and living. Our highly-praised liturgical tradition is for
the most part unknown and unlived by great numbers of
our people, and all too often by the official teachers and
professors of the faith as well. Our claims to universal and
catholic churchly being and life, consciousness and mission,
are for the most part obscured and denied by the crudest
and basest expressions of ethnicism, nationalism and simple
human pride and vanity, both in the traditional "homelands" of Orthodoxy and most certainly in the so-called
"diaspora"—a notoriously unchristian term which betrays in
its very utterance how far we are in practice from what, by
God's grace, we still somehow retain in theory. Our personal and ecclesiastical relationships with each other, and
with our fellow-Christians as well, are to a large degree
riddled with ignorance, mistrust, competition, suspicion and
simple self-service. The unholy triad of creaturely self-
destruction—pride, fear and envy—are all too often the
spirits which enslave our relationships with each other and
our fellow men, instead of the blessed trinity of virtues

inspired by God's Spirit which bless us to be free and honest in our dealings: humility, courage and self-abandoning love. To say these things is painful and embarassing. Yet these things must be said because they are true, and at least we in America are perishing because of them and are thereby failing in our mission of witness and service as Orthodox Christians and human beings.

One of my teachers and fathers in the faith once said to me that he considers this last half century as a certain "moment of truth" for Orthodoxy in the world, the time of its "final examination" in the modern era. He said that the question facing Orthodox Christians right now is the most basic of questions: *to be or not to be!* We have hope today that the Orthodox Church and the Orthodox faith will continue to be. We have this hope because we believe that God is faithful and will not leave Himself and His Church without witnesses and servants. We know that there are some in the Church already chosen for this end. We even dare to say that we see some who are not formally members of the Orthodox Church living and acting as the Church commands all people to do in her scriptures, sacraments and saints. And we rejoice in our ability to make such a claim. For there are those, certainly within the Orthodox Church, whom we can identify as chosen of God to be witnesses and servants of the "sanity" of His people. They are accomplishing their calling as this calling is always accomplished: by their courageous and unassuming fidelity to God's will in little things; by their ability to sanctify and transfigure the everyday life in this world by the grace and glory of God; by their willingness to suffer, silently and unspectacularly, for all that is good and true, beautiful and right, in the life of human beings as provided by God. They are the "holy remnant," the poor in spirit and the pure in heart who, by their wounds of body and soul, are fulfilling "what is lacking in Christ's afflictions for the sake of His body, the Church" (Col. 1:24). They do not live in any one part of the world. Golgotha is everywhere. In the communist countries, militantly atheistic, where basic human rights are denied and where Christian life is degraded and humiliated by being locked up in cultic temples, the form of their witness and service befits their conditions. In the so-called "free world" of the West, where the many "reductions" of man run rampant and where Christians so often hold the forms of churchly life while denying its substance and power, their suffering witness and service has other expressions. In other parts of the world, God's witnesses and servants act in their own unique ways. But Christ is being crucified and raised in people everywhere who by their "sanity" inspired by God are insuring "sanity" for us all, if only we can see it and embrace it in grateful repentance. Because of these people there is hope for us and for God's world.

Now to Him who by the power at work within us is able to do far more than all that we ask or think, to Him be glory in the Church and in Christ Jesus to all generations (Eph. 3:20-21).